MW00777960

Black Theology and Pedagogy

Black Religion/Womanist Thought/Social Justice
Series Editors Dwight N. Hopkins and Linda E. Thomas
Published by Palgrave Macmillan

Black Theology and Pedagogy

Noel Leo Erskine

First published in 2008 by
PALGRAVE MACMILLAN®
in the US—a division of St. Martin's Press LLC,
175 Fifth Avenue, New York, NY 10010.

Where this book is distributed in the UK, Europe and the rest of the world,
this is by Palgrave Macmillan, a division of Macmillan Publishers Limited,
registered in England, company number 785998, of Houndmills,
Basingstoke, Hampshire RG21 6XS.

Palgrave Macmillan is the global academic imprint of the above companies
and has companies and representatives throughout the world.

Palgrave® and Macmillan® are registered trademarks in the United States,
the United Kingdom, Europe and other countries.

ISBN-13: 978–1–4039–7740–3
ISBN-10: 1–4039–7740–2

Library of Congress Cataloging-in-Publication Data is available from the
Library of Congress.

A catalogue record for this book is available from the British Library.

Design by Newgen Imaging Systems (P) Ltd., Chennai, India.

First edition: August 2008

10 9 8 7 6 5 4 3 2 1

Printed in the United States of America.

In memory of my father The Rev. U.N. Leo Erskine
My first mentor of pedagogy and theology

Contents

Preface

This book had its genesis in a three-year consultation on Pedagogy and Theology at the Wabash Center for Teaching and Learning during summers 1996–1999. There were about a dozen of us theologians who met under the leadership of Bill Placher, who pressed us to tease out the implications of our construction of theology as source and resource for excellence in teaching and learning. One of the advantages of this consultation was each of us had the opportunity to present a perspective on theology and pedagogy and receive critical comments from members of the consultation. I would like to pay special tribute to Serene Jones and Miroslav Volf with whom I discussed many of the central ideas for this project, especially in its early stages.

I am also grateful for a research luncheon with "The Dark Tower," a group of faculty and administrators from the Institute of the Liberal Arts at Emory University, who engaged me in critical dialogue around the salient ideas offered in this text. My colleagues in the Graduate Division of Religion at Emory were also instructive in the fall conversation in which I shared the central ideas of this book. Expressions of thanks are due to Wendy Farley, Mark Jordan, Ian McFarlane, Walt Lowe, and Joy McDougal.

To the editors of this series Linda Thomas and Dwight Hopkins I am indebted for much feedback from the original draft of the manuscript. Others who helped me think through several of the ideas presented in this text are: Mary Elizabeth Moore, Theodore Brelsford, and Anthony Pinn. John Snarey with whom I have had several discussions about this project contributed greatly.

Anthony Reddie at the Queens Foundation for Ecumenical Theological Education, Birmingham, United Kingdom has been an invaluable colleague in helping me work through the connections between pedagogy and its ecclesial context.

A special word of gratitude to my students, both in systematic theology and cross-cultural theologies, for many insights gleaned from class presentations. Many thanks to Estelle Archibold who helped with the bibliography and Alvelyn Sanders who assisted with editing.

The central question this book engages is: what are the implications for pedagogy in the classroom and in ecclesial settings if texts and contexts that have been excluded become essential for teaching and learning.? Because I write and reflect on this question from my social location in the African Diaspora, the reader will note that I make the case for the inclusion of the Black community in contexts of teaching and learning. The scriptures enjoin us to "honor our parents" and from a Black perspective this means our ancestors, our "sheroes," and heroes, our mothers, sisters, and of course our brothers and fathers. To refine and rephrase the question with which this book is concerned, I ask: What would it look like to "teach in Black?" that is not only to use token texts by Black authors but to allow these texts in the context of Black culture and history to shape the questions that are generative.

For many of my colleagues the attempt to teach in Black is comparable to struggle with the cross of Blackness. The immediate reaction to the cross is flight. The cross frightens and repulses us and raises the question of what would "discipleship to the cross" (the Black experience) entail as a pedagogical strategy? This question is important not only for White people who struggle with appropriate texts to use and how to engage Black issues in class, but also for Black scholars who seek to demonstrate their proficiency in Euro-American culture and thereby marginalize Black history and culture.

The good news for both White and Black persons who engage the cross of Blackness is the discovery that the cross heals and transforms. Black is beautiful.

It is my hope that this book identifies and isolates several of the unique contributions that Black and womanist theologies bring to excellence in teaching and learning. In many ways I am beginning a conversation that I hope others will join.

NOEL LEO ERSKINE
Emory University

Introduction

This book seeks to look at the emergence of Black theology as a discipline within the academy, and investigate how Black theology may serve as a resource for excellence in teaching and learning. This is of interest, because Black theology engages pedagogy to note that in the first decade of its development, all the theologians were men and it did not occur to these Black male theologians that women, particularly Black women were excluded. Although the impetus for the construction and articulation of this theology was the exclusion of Black people by White religionists, Black theologians were careful not to adopt the exclusionary approach of White religionists in relation to White men but included them both in the exposition and analysis of its major themes and arguments. Unlike White theologians, who excluded Black people from their theological discourse, Black theologians were inclusive in relation to the White academy. I find it instructive for pedagogy in classroom and church that Black theologians refused to pattern God-talk from the White model of exclusion, but have insisted that if theology is to be in the service of creating and sustaining a compassionate and diverse community, then the stranger must be embraced both in the academy and church.

Taking my cue from Black theologians, I would like to examine what it means in the classroom to include the stranger, the person of a different race, ethnicity, religion, and culture. Yet, the converse was equally true. In including the stranger, Black theologians excluded the person of the same race, ethnicity, religion, and history. Black women were excluded. While the outsider from another race, ethnicity, and culture was included, the insider from the same race, ethnicity, and culture was excluded. We must inquire as to whether one reason for the exclusion of Black women by Black theologians had to do with the notion of sameness. Could it be that because Black women were of the same race, culture, and in many cases religion they were ignored as

Black theologians failed to recognize that sameness does not mean identical? While they saw White men as different and construed difference in terms of unknowability, they failed to see difference in Black women in terms of transcendence. I would like to investigate to what extent Black theologians, in making peace with immanence that confronted them in Black women, overlooked issues of transcendence. We must inquire, what does it mean to affirm the transcendence of the person of the same race, ethnicity, culture, and religion? How may we discover that transcendence is hidden in immanence?

Other themes to be explored are the investigation of whether there are continuities between the classroom and the Black church. Is the space created in the classroom transgressive space in which all are permitted to risk their own voice and identity, as is often the case in the Black church? Should good teaching and learning include testimonies, stories of resistance and adventure? James Cone, in his important book *Risks of Faith*[1] and bell hooks in *Teaching to Transgress*[2] provide important help in this discussion. Also of importance is the article by Black theologian J. Deotis Roberts "Liberating Theological Education: Can our Seminaries Be Saved?"[3] in which he contends that in theological education we must do more than ask about the continuities between church and classroom. Rather, we must be concerned about the cries of the oppressed in our societies and the classroom. Because the cry that exudes from the oppressed is the cry for liberation, according to Roberts we must inquire if education is for liberation and reconciliation. It is interesting to note that in February 1983, when this article by Roberts was published, he did not identify the subservient place of Black women in church and academy as a need for liberation. This is especially poignant since he wrote as president of the Interdenominational Theological Center in Atlanta. Roberts called attention for the need in the academy and the church to ground pedagogy in Black culture and history and resist the urge to be anti-intellectual as Black people accept themselves as made in the image of God. He frames the issue for us:

> When blacks excavate their African roots, they participate in a holistic view of reality. When we are at home with ourselves and our culture, and not trying to be like somebody else, we are holistic in thought and faith. We are never liberated until we make this discovery. What this means is that we blacks have a real contribution to make to theology and the Christian movement—if we can be set free. Thus, the first item on our agenda may be the psychological freedom to think and believe out of our own culture and history.[4]

Roberts is quite helpful as a Black theologian in giving us a feel for the central questions on the agenda of Black theologians in the second decade of Black theology's advent as an academic discipline and a sense of the contribution Black theology could make in the classroom.

According to Roberts, Black theology is significant for pedagogy because Black theology offers pedagogy a holistic worldview in its affirmation of the unity of body and soul, secular and sacred, piety and activism. Further, Black theology inspires pedagogy in that it points to the Black community's "ability to transmute personal and group suffering into moral victory.... The tendency to surround each other with love and community in tough times is to be cherished."[5] Roberts reminds us that theological education seen within the prism of liberation and reconciliation must be priestly and prophetic. It must be priestly as it seeks to conserve values of self-love and renounce the penchant for imitation. Theological education must also be prophetic as it places values of social justice and human worth at the center of the curriculum and life together in the seminary community. "Black seminarians at predominantly white seminaries are asking to be recognized as persons of worth. They are calling for attention to curriculum offerings more in keeping with their future ministry.... There is a worsening of the situation for blacks at white seminaries as resources decline. Since concern for the black agenda was never central to most seminaries, the shortage of funds seems to be the answer to the prayers of those who would maintain the status quo on race relations."[6]

Black theologians during the first two decades of the development of Black theology mirrored the position of Roberts. The main difference was a matter of emphasis and methodology not a fundamental shift in substance or focus. For example, Cecil Wayne Cone's *The Identity Crisis in Black Theology*[7] was a theological quarrel with his brother James Cone in which he challenged his brother to give priority to Black religion in the articulation of Black theology. But there was no quarrel concerning the common task at hand, they were agreed that the central theological problem was racism. And part of what this meant was they would engage White theologians in the academy and church as they challenged structures of oppression that were organized against the human flourishing of oppressed people.

Pedagogy and the Black Community

Black theologians were agreed that the first truth was truth about the Black community, the recounting of their stories, and the affirmation of their heritage. J. Deotis Roberts would join the quarrel with James Cone as to whether or not the hermeneutical key was liberation or reconciliation, but they were agreed that the problem was racism. To identify the problem was to begin to press for liberation and reconciliation. They sought to free their people with truth as they engaged those who within church and academy would compromise their humanity. Although the problem, as Black theologians stated, had to do with White theologians within the academy and church who rendered Black people invisible, they refused to pattern their approach to pedagogy and God-talk after the method of exclusion adopted and embraced by White academicians and theologians within the church. Black theologians observed that if theology would be in the service of pedagogy in church and academy as it sought to fashion a compassionate and diverse community, then the neighbor as stranger and critic had to be embraced.

Because Black theology is Christian theology and affirms the church as the home of theology, it begins to make sense that with the influence of the Black church in the background and quite often in the foreground, the church's reference to the Biblical injunction to be hospitable to strangers, Hebrews 13:1–2, would be taken seriously. James Cone in his *God of the Oppressed* informs us that he was licensed to preach at age sixteen. I would not be surprised if this invitation to be hospitable to strangers would have been part of the ethos in the African Methodist Episcopal Church in which he was reared in Bearden, Arkansas. There was always an element of surprise in the Black church that God would treat us the way we treated strangers. There was no attempt in the Black church to practice reverse discrimination and no one exemplifies this better than Martin Luther King, Jr. Cone in his important book *Martin and Malcolm and America: A Dream or a Nightmare*[8] points to the role of the Civil Rights Movement in the United States under the leadership of King as indispensable for the visioning and articulation of Black theology. Martin Luther King Jr. indicates that the Black church's understanding of what it means to be human in church as in the academy is an outgrowth of their understanding of who God is. Because God is a God of Love who is generous to all God's children and does not privilege one group of children over another, it means that all God's children have virtue and inherent worth, even if some of God's children advocate segregation and racism.

King would insist that every human being by virtue of being human has inherent worth, and no person, society, or culture has the right to deny his or her dignity. The bottom line for King was that racism was a sin against God. Love for God meant working to dismantle the very fabric of racism. But in spite of the human condition soiled by racism, every human being may claim respect because God loves him/her. "The worth of an individual does not lie in the measure of his intellect, racial origin, or social position. Human worth lies in relatedness to God. An individual has value because he has value to God."[9] Because God's love is the basis of the worth of human beings, it means that all persons are of equal worth. There is no theological or biblical basis for regarding White people as superior to Black people. King echoes the Black church's perspective:

> Our Hebraic-Christian tradition refers to this inherent dignity of man in the Biblical term the image of God. This innate worth referred to in the phrase the image of God is universally shared in equal portions by all men. There is no graded scale of essential worth: there is no divine right of one race which differs from the divine right of another. Every human being has etched in his personality the indelible stamp of the creator.[10]

It is of first importance to note that Cone, like his mentor King, could insist on a relationship of love for the critic and neighbor who sought to render Black people invisible and in some instances to destroy Black people. For both King and Cone there was an indissoluble relationship between love and justice. King while learning this in the Black church gave it theological exposition and analysis in his dissertation for Boston University on the thought of Henry Nelson Wieman and Paul Tillich.

From Tillich, King learned that any responsible attempt to practice love in church, society, or the academy has to take seriously the inter-relatedness of love, power and justice. King would often remind his hearers that love without power was anemic and power without love was calculated. Students of the Civil Rights Movement will remember that King was forced to engage this analysis because of the leaders of the SNCC, who pointed out to King that in his constant plea for Black people to confront White brutality with nonviolent resistance, to turn the other cheek, he was calling on Black people to love White people without demanding that Black people practice justice toward themselves in learning to love themselves. The students contended that there was nothing that hurt oppressed people as too much love for others, especially when the intent of others was to destroy them. This was an important lesson for King and Black theologians: the danger of always loving self last and often last meant not at all as one never got around to finding time or space to love self. The students taught King, and Cone insisted in his attempt to reach out to the stranger that love as it engages power must insist on justice. Both King and Cone understood justice as the essence of love. But the mistake that both King and Cone made was seeing justice only in terms of the analysis of the structures of alienation and oppression.

Although intellectually, King understood and Cone reminds us that an examination of relations of love, power, and justice must begin with justice, these theologians did not practice love and accord justice to women who were close at hand. This was why in the case of King, women were often not affirmed in leadership positions in the running of the Civil Rights Movement. Although women were the most vulnerable, they were often invisible when opportunities for leadership in the Movement presented itself and when given an opportunity to lead they were not affirmed. It stands to reason then that there were no women among Black theologians in the first few decades of the development of Black theology. Further, the names of women who were active in the Civil Rights Movement do not come readily to mind as are the names of men who identified with Martin Luther King, Jr. Most students of the Civil Rights Movement are familiar with the names of Jessie Jackson, Ralph David Abernathy, John Lewis, Andrew Young, C.T. Vivian, and James Lawson. But if asked to name women who were identified with the Movement they stop at Coretta Scott King, the wife of the slain Civil Rights leader. There is a sense in which women were invisible in the Movement. Not that they were not there, because Rosa Parks started the trail that led to the Movement. As someone has said, "She sat down so that Martin Luther King, Jr. could stand up." Further, it was the Women's Political Council at Alabama State College, led by Jo Ann Robinson, that got the leaflets out to advertise the bus boycott. Besides, both the jails and freedom rides were crowded with women. Women who had leadership roles in the Movement were Dorothy Cotton, the director of the Citizenship Education Program (CEP); Septima Clark, who was director of the workshops of CEP; and Ella Baker, who organized the Southern Christian Leadership Conference. (SCLC) and served as acting director for a short while. Commenting on Baker's tenure as acting director, Cone states:

> Although she served as its "acting director," most of the male preachers were uneasy with her presence because she did not exhibit the "right attitude" [read "submissiveness"?] which they expected from women,

an expectation no doubt shaped by the role of women in their churches. Ella Baker's tenure with SCLC was relatively brief (though longer than she expected), largely because of her conflicts with King and others regarding their attitude toward women and their leadership style built around the charisma of one person—Martin Luther King, Jr. Baker preferred the group-centered leadership developed by SNCC, whose founding she initiated.[11]

Both King and Cone because of their first commitment to analysis of structures of domination and oppression were able to make room for the stranger, the person of a different race, ethnicity, and class as love was translated as truth confronting power and justice was viewed as an analysis of structures of oppression. In embracing the stranger, the person of a different race, they neglected the most vulnerable among them—the Black woman. This is surprising because both Black theology as articulated by Cone and certainly by J. Deotis Roberts and King's articulation of the Beloved Community has the openness that provides for the inclusion of women. The exclusion of women points to the gap between theory and practice, oughtness and isness.

Black and Christian

One of the challenges that faces Black theology at this point of our discussion as theology seeks to engage pedagogy is to ask in what way if any is Black theology Christian theology and further what is the appropriate response of Black theology to racism in church and academy? The first question regarding the status of Black theology in relation to Christian theology becomes important as we recall that in the articulation of Black theology, Black power played a central role. Issues of self-determination and self-acceptance were crucial, as lessons from Black history and Black culture sought to illuminate the ethical response of Black people to a racist environment that was marginalizing and rendering them invisible. Black people had to live with a past and present reality in which many White people denied their existence as children of God. This is certainly one reason why the majority of Black Christians are outside the White church and it became important for the Black community to found and establish Black institutions of higher learning. Martin Luther King, Jr. reminded us that 11 am on Sundays is the most racist hour in America as Black and White congregations gathered for worship. For better or for worse, we are separated. The turn of Black church/Black theology to

Black power was to identify the root cause of the problem: racism. As Black theology engages pedagogy we must acknowledge that the primordial springs that nurture and nourish Black existence are different from that of White people.

Black theology reminds us of the difference in the long history of suffering in the American South that shaped the soul of Black people. As W.E.B. Du Bois taught us that to be Black in America is to be African and American at the same time. Black theology as it engages pedagogy must deal with this twoness. Black theology teaches us that the wellsprings that replenish Black life are different from that of White people. To be Black in America is to live in the tension between freedom and bondage. The overcoming of the many forms of bondage that afflict the Black community is not found in sacrificial love that insists on loving self last. The truth is that this has always been part of our problem because last means never finding time or the courage to love self. Black theology coupled with Black power instructs Black people to accept their uniqueness. As J. Deotis Roberts admonished us earlier, the challenge is the freedom not to imitate White values and the White way of life as the way forward.

This means that Black theology seeks to become Christian theology on two fronts. On the one hand it insists on the primacy of community. It is not enough for the response to racism to be private and personal, but it issues forth out of the life of the Black community. Echoing John Mbiti in *African Religions and Philosophy*, the response from within the church and academy should be "I am because we are. It is because we are that I am." To be human is to be in community. The second challenge, as Black theology seeks to become Christian theology, is that Black theology does not merely seek to interpret Black existence, but to transform institutional life in such a way that the Black community becomes a window through which other peoples can get a glimpse of what it looks like to become more like Christ. It is precisely at this point that Black theology instructs pedagogy in terms of its Christian responsibility in a racist school and a racist church. As Black theology informs pedagogy, the challenge facing Blacks in the classroom and in the church is how to be Black and Christian at the same time. A part of what this means is that loyalty to Christ does not obviate loyalty to ones cultural and historical legacy. The Black Christian acknowledges the legacy of slavery and Jim Crowism, the history of racial segregation and oppression in America. The struggle in these multiple contexts is for liberation and reconciliation that simultaneously accepts where Black people are and charts the way forward. The way forward is to dream of transformation in church and classroom. It is in this context that Blacks are allowed and given the right to speak their own words, to name their own reality, and to dream new dreams.

Learning from the Stranger

Perhaps there is a sense in which Black theology's turn to the stranger was a turn toward dreams of reconciliation and eschatological hope. Hope for wholeness and healing in race relations. In any case, it is instructive that a look at Cone's *Black Theology and Black Power* indicates Black theology's commitment to White ways of talking about God, humanity, and the world. Cone engages White thinkers as diverse as Emil Brunner, Rudolf Bultmann, Dietrich Bonhoeffer, Gunther Bornkham, Billy Graham, Karl Jasper, Soren Kierkegaard, and Richard Niebuhr, to name a few. Cone informs the reader that he was introduced to White thinkers in seminary and graduate school and wrote his dissertation on Karl Barth's anthropology. What is instructive in Cone's turn to White thinkers is a willingness to be in conversation with the critic and stranger in spite of the White stranger's commitment to humiliate and to render Black people invisible. Cone puts it this way:

> When I graduated with a Bachelor of Arts degree from Philander Smith and was accepted at Garrett theological Seminary in Evanston, Illinois (now Garrett-Evangelical), I was a little naïve, for I was sure that things would be different. I had internalized the myth that blacks were treated equally "up north," but that myth was demolished for me in less than one day in Evanston and Garrett. Although racism at Garrett and in Evanston was not as obvious as in Arkansas, I believe that it was much more vicious, especially in terms of the structural brutality inflicted upon black dignity and self-confidence. I almost did not survive past my first quarter at Garrett, making all C's from professors who told me that I deserved less. This was a common experience for the few blacks allowed to matriculate at Garrett during the late 1950's and early '60s.[12]

This was the experience of many Black persons who dared to darken the academic halls of White institutions of higher learning also in the 1970s and early 1980s throughout the United States. This was one reason for the formation of Black Caucuses in many White institutions throughout the United States. Black Caucuses provided Black sacred space where Black people did not have to struggle against the White myth of being inferior but were free to allow Black history and culture to illuminate their being together in community and their discourse about what it means to be human in an environment in which Black dignity and Black self-respect are constantly under attack. It is also of interest to note that in 1970 Black professors of religion throughout the United States formed The Society for the Study of Black Religion that was aimed at providing Black sacred space for theological discourse. The fact that this Society is still in existence and numbers over one hundred colleagues calls attention to the need for a creative context in the academy where Black people will be taken seriously as they allow their history and culture and the Black religious experience to illuminate theological discourse.

Perhaps Cone's turn to White colleagues in the academy is one way of acknowledging the need for the creation of sacred space where respect and dignity are accorded all participants and Black people and others do not have to fear "receiving all Cs." It is to the credit of Black theologians that the door has always been cracked for communication and dialogue with the person of a different race. In spite of the history of oppression, Cone has always insisted that the "conversation matters," there is much to learn from the stranger. Cone seems to suggest that strangers are our neighbors and that God has given us neighbors for us to respect, safeguard their dignity, and learn from them.

This is an important key as Black theology informs pedagogy, and seeks to create Black sacred space for conversation informed by dignity and respect. While I am not sure Black theology as articulated by Cone is able to go all the way as instructed by Leviticus 19:33–34, it is quite clear in its embrace of the stranger that it is headed in the right direction

> When a stranger resides with you in your land, you shall not do him wrong.
>
> The stranger who resides with you shall be to you as the native among you, and you shall love him as yourself; for you were aliens in the land of Egypt: I am the Lord your God.[13]

What lessons are there in this text that may guide us in the embrace of the stranger? Are we able to honor the Biblical injunction to love the stranger as we love self? It is precisely at this point the sacrament of hospitality becomes crucial for pedagogical practices. What would the practice of love for self and neighbor look like in the classroom?

The Biblical injunction seeks to take us further than Black theology is able to. It seeks to engage in emancipatory pedagogy as the Biblical text encourages us to set goals, and engage in practices that foster a liberating consciousness. Frederick Douglas said, "We should not expect crops without tilling the soil." We should not expect members of a class to learn to love self and neighbor without participating in the telling of their own stories. It stands as a pedagogical maxim that we cannot free ourselves with practices that are anchored in the narrative of others. As members of a class we must be willing to place our stories in conversation with others. Listening to strangers is at the same time a willingness to take ourselves seriously. Students often ask concerning contexts in which they feel devalued: "How should I respond in a class that defines me as C?" The student as stranger identifies the tension between what she knows she is essentially, and the way her context portrays her. The way forward is love for self that includes the practice of justice toward self. This means an attitude of affirmation and a struggle to explode the myths that marginalize and circumscribe one as a member of a class. Students should be encouraged not to respond in the way they are defined. The student has to rebel, has to "talk back." The other must be encountered as a person. This is part of what it means to teach and learn after the advent of Black theology.

Black Theology and the Black Woman

While Black theology took pains in addressing the stranger, it overlooked the Black woman as friend, mother, and sister who was close at hand. Cone in a confessional note places the issue before us:

> Although Black women represent more than one-half of the population in the Black community and 75 percent in the Black Church, their experience has not been visibly present in the development of Black Theology. For the most part, Black male theologians have remained conspicuously silent on feminist theology generally and Black women in particular. We have spoken of the Black religious experience as if it consisted only of our male experience with no distinctive contribution from Black women.[14]

Cone offers suggestions regarding the silence of Black theologians in reference to the invisibility of Black women in the Black theological enterprise. According to Cone, there are some Black male theologians "who are blatantly sexist" and thereby reflect the dominant culture in this regard. "Others regard the problem of racism as the basic injustice and say that feminism is a middle-class White woman's issue. Still others make the controversial claim that the Black woman is already liberated.... Among professional theologians and preachers as well as seminary and university students, few Black men seem to care about the pain our Black sisters claim that we inflict on them with our sexist behavior. If we expect to be taken seriously about our claim to love them, must not our love express itself in our capacity to hear their cry of pain and to experience with them their mental and physical suffering?"[15]

In the attempt to connect with Black women who have been rendered invisible by Black theologians, Cone sounds condescending as he suggests that Black theologians should show Black women some love by listening to their cries and be willing to embrace their pain. Cone is not yet willing to deal with sexism in Black theology: the fact that Black women are excluded as thinkers, as theologians in their own right. Cone misses an opportunity to point to the structural relationship between racism and sexism. His preoccupation with racism seems to provide blinders that prevent him from taking with full seriousness the interconnectedness of racism, sexism, and classism. Another way of identifying this difficult place in which Cone stands is to acknowledge his failure to sufficiently point to the relationship between the particular and the universal in theological discourse and in classroom practice. "As is always the case, it is difficult for people to recognize the significance of a particular form of experience when it does not arise from their own lives. My attempt to recognize the importance of women's experience in theology is found in the classes I teach at Union.... My earlier books ignored the issue of sexism; I believe now that such an exclusion was and is a gross distortion of the theological meaning of the Christian faith."[16] While Cone is correct in not wanting to subsume the particular in the universal and thereby lose the specificity of his analysis of racism, the challenge is how to allow the particular to provide a window through which others are able to see that their oppression and need for liberation is taken seriously. To respond to the exclusion of Black women from Black theological discourse with the assertion that Black men must love them and listen to their cries is not yet to take them with sufficient seriousness.

This seems to be the assessment of womanist theologian Jacquelyn Grant in her important article "Black Theology and the Black Woman." Grant begins by pointing out the importance of a theological analysis that honors the interrelationship of racism, sexism, and classism. To highlight any one of these perspectives is to refuse to press for authentic liberation. Grant enquires: "Where are black women in Black theology? They are in fact, invisible....In examining Black Theology it is necessary to make one of two assumptions: (1) either Black women have no place in the enterprise, or (2) Black men are capable of speaking for us. Both of these assumptions are false and need to be discarded. They arise out of a male-dominated culture which restricts women to certain areas of the society. In such a culture men are given the warrant to speak for women."[17] Grant exposes Black theology and the main reasons for the invisibility of Black women in Black theology. According to theologian Grant one word gets to the heart of the matter: patriarchy. Patriarchy is the subordination of women to male worldview. The attempt of men to act and speak for women. Patriarchy manifests itself in the notion that men are superior to women because women are given to emotionality and intuition while men are given to reason and intellect. "Just as White women formerly had no place in White theology—except as the receptors of White men's theological interpretations—Black women have had no place in the development of Black theology. By self-appointment, or by the sinecure of a male dominated society. Black men have deemed it proper to speak for the entire Black community, male and female."[18]

Professor Grant is very helpful in describing a great deal of the practice that informs teacher student relationship in the classroom. "Just as White women formerly had no place in White theology—except as receptors of White men's theological interpretations....," Black theology in particular, as it relates to the Black woman and White theology in general as it engages pedagogy, is guilty of ways of relating and instructing in the classroom that does not honor the contributions of its participants. According to Grant, Black and White theologians deny women the opportunity and fail to affirm their ability to think theologically. This is a problem in many classrooms in departments of religion and in theological seminaries that instructors whether White or Black men tend to arrogate to themselves this ability to speak for women and thereby speak for God. Grant on the one hand faults Black theologians for the sin of imitation. "Black men must ask themselves a difficult question. How can a White society characterized by Black enslavement, colonialism, and imperialism provide the normative conception of women for Black society?[19]

Grant proposes another problem that informs pedagogy. If theology proffered by White theologians, which undergirds the patriarchal structure of society, is taken over by Black men, why should Black women think that this could be for their liberation? "If Black men have accepted those structures, is there any reason to believe that the theology written by Black men would be any more liberating of Black women than White theology was for White women?"[20] The way forward is to put "new wine in new wineskins" (Luke 5:38). Grant reminds us that although Black theology purports to be a theology of the Black religious experience, the problem has been that Black women's experience was excluded. It is precisely at this point Grant points out that something new is needed.

Pedagogy as Invitation to Love God

In her classic text *White Women's Christ and Black Women's Jesus*, Grant points out that the oppression of women in church and society lead women to ask as their central question, "What has Jesus Christ to do with the status of women in church and society?" This question is a paraphrase of the question Jesus asked his disciples, "Who do you say that I am?" Grant indicates that for a long time men have sought to answer this question for women, but this must not continue, as women have to answer this from their own experience. In the past, women have allowed men to say who Jesus is for them, thereby denying the validity of their own experience. The problem is not merely that men have suggested answers to this question, but they have sought to give definitive answers.

> Since man is limited by his social context and interests, Jesus Christ has been defined within the narrow parameters of male consciousness. That is to say, the social context of the men who have been theologizing has been the normative criterion upon which theological interpretations have been based. What this has meant is that Jesus Christ consistently has been used to give legitimacy to the customary beliefs regarding the status of women.[21]

Grant calls attention to the importance of Black women's experience as a pedagogical resource. The importance of women's experience as source and resource for education cannot be overestimated as it places women in a position to teach and to initiate an exodus from traditions that thwart their human flourishing.

It is precisely at this point that Grant's emphasis on women's experience as a basis for talk about God and pedagogy proffers an ethic of care as the next step. Care for self and neighbor. The focus on care for self and neighbor highlights pedagogy as an invitation to love God. We noted earlier in Leviticus 19 that pedagogy as love for God included the commandment to love the stranger. And in Mark 12:30–31 as Jesus paraphrases Deuteronomy 6:4–5 he points out that love for God includes love for self and neighbor. It seems to me then that with Black theology's emphasis on love for strangers as it tackles the stubborn reality of racism, and with womanist theology's focus on the need to isolate and identify women's experience as a source for talk about God and pedagogy as it takes on patriarchy, we are led in a new way to engage pedagogy as love for God. Love for God includes the critic as stranger, self, and neighbor. Each is invited to bear witness from experience of what it means to practice the love of God.

I

Pedagogy and Black Community

An appropriate starting point for the study of pedagogy and Black community is to acknowledge that the NAACP's legal strategies bore fruit when in 1954 the Supreme Court overturned school segregation in the nation. The Court ended its "separate but equal" doctrine and admitted that inherent in legal segregation was the notion of Black inferiority that made suspect the education offered in this setting. It did not take much imagination to conclude that education offered in this context could render irreparable damage to the self-esteem of students, especially Black students. Education took on a new sense of importance as schools throughout the nation were ordered to desegregate in order that the racist structure of education would take the back seat, and a new confidence and sense of self could emerge among Black students. The Court's order was an attempt to reverse over three hundred years of discrimination and second-class citizenship meted out to Black people by the dominant culture and society. Black inferiority had become a way of life for many who were forced through Jim Crow laws to drink at separate water fountains, sit in the back of public transportations, have no protection against police brutality, refusal of access to many educational institutions, and in many cases be subject to harassment and lynching by White hate groups such as the Ku Klux Klan.

What the Court did not foresee was that a change in educational practices presumed a change in relationship between Black and White people. The truth is that the all White Court perceived that leadership to change the educational system, which placed Black people at an enormous disadvantage, had to come from White people since they had power backed by law enforcement. Although many Black people welcomed the action of the Court they were powerless to claim the equality that they perceived the Court intended for them. Black existence was marked by powerlessness for a very long time.

King's Response to the Court

Rosa Parks in her refusal to give up her seat in a Montgomery bus the following year indicated that Black people had drawn the conclusion that if segregation in schools was wrong then segregation in any place was wrong. Mrs. Parks gave feet to the quiet revolution that aimed to usher in the age of integration. With the help of Martin Luther King, Jr. the quiet revolution sparked by Parks provided an occasion for the Black community to join protest in many areas of life to defeat segregation, racism, and the sense of powerlessness that plagued the Black community. What the Civil Rights Movement did for the nation in the ensuing years was help us see the racial divide between White and Black people and the visioning and articulation of King's dream for community.

The order from the Supreme Court sparked interest in equality among many Black people and a sense of entitlement to educational institutions without reference to color. King and his Movement began to dream of integration, but the protests and burning of cities that followed revealed the alienation that existed between Black and White people. Something happened when Rosa Parks refused to give up her seat on the Montgomery city bus. A new awareness of equal rights, self-determination, and freedom took hold of the Black community. "Every success of King contributed to the black man's increasing need for being himself. Finally, from the frustrations of youth and also from their impetuousness came the catalyst that was to force the new awareness to surface. Out of the dark bowels of the South; out of the black belt in which the black man had suffered the most, been crushed, defeated, and killed; out of Mississippi came the cry of liberation, Black power! Black Power!"[1]

The cry for Black power resounded across the nation in Black communities as young radicals in the Civil Rights Movement kindled the imagination of the Black community in contending that love without power is anemic. They argued that the critical need in the community was not just love for the critic or person of another race, but power to effect change and embrace values that are important for human flourishing. The harsh truth was that if the Black community was to take on segregation and make the order of the Supreme Court a reality, and in King's own mind move toward integration between Black and

White people, love needed to be informed and supported by the power of self-determination.

The Black church responded to the cry of the students when on July 31, 1966, the National Committee of Negro Churchmen stated: "We are faced now with a situation where conscienceless power meets powerless conscience, threatening the very foundation of the nation."[2] In the initial stage, King was uncomfortable with the language of Black power as he saw clearly the possibility for it to further separate Black and White people. However, toward the end of his life he wore a button that read "Black is beautiful." King wanted to couch the language of power within the context of his understanding of what it meant to be human. One of his concerns was that if love without power is anemic then power without love could be calculated. His training as a preacher and a theologian equipped him for the task of conjoining love and power and he was more comfortable at this than in dealing with what he perceived to be the incendiary notion of Black power. King observed that a large part of what it meant to be human was the power to choose where one lives, goes to school, as well as how one survives given the racist culture that made America sick.

King anchored his understanding of community in an explication of his understanding of God. Every person, Black or White is worthy of respect because God loves her/him. "The worth of an individual does not lie in the measure of his intellect, his racial origin, or social position. Human worth lies in relatedness to God. An individual has value because he has value to God."[3]

King anchors his view of the worth of persons in the Biblical and theological understanding of the image of God. Because God's grace is the basis of the worth of human beings, it means that all persons are of equal worth. There is no theological or biblical basis for regarding Western people as superior to other peoples or for regarding White people as superior to Black people. The image of God is universally shared in an equal way by all persons. Every person has stamped in his/her personality the indelible image of God. King states the issue for us:

> Our Hebraic-Christian tradition refers to this inherent dignity of man in the Biblical term the image of God. This innate worth referred to in the phrase the image of God is universally shared in equal portions by all men. There is no graded scale of essential worth, there is no divine right of one race which differs from the divine right of another. Every human being has etched in his personality the indelible stamp of the creator.[4]

King was not at this point making an argument for Black theology or for Black power. On the contrary, he was making an argument for the primacy of the human community.

One aim was the desegregation of public institutions. As far as King was concerned there was no special value in being a Black or White community. Black people were being marginalized and he sought to articulate a vision that would bring them into the mainstream and make the move from segregation to integration. His teaching about what it means to be human was based on his understanding of God's love for all. Failure to view persons in the light of the image of God would run the risk of treating persons as things—as means rather than ends in themselves. King borrows Martin Buber's language and speaks of the danger of reducing persons to an "I-it" relationship. "The tragedy of segregation is that it treats men as means rather than ends, and thereby reduces them to things rather than persons.... Segregation substitutes an 'I-it' relationship for an 'I-thou' relationship."[5] In spite of our view of community, whether our preference is for community that reflects the integration or segregation model, King's caution of reducing persons to the status of "I-it" rather than "I-thou" is revealing of one's understanding of personhood. It raises the question of what we view as decisive in our attempt to talk about the place of persons in community.

King's understanding of community is anchored in his view of God. He felt that this approach would safeguard an emphasis on the individual and push toward a commitment to community. The problem as King saw it was that to press for a Black community would not make any advancement on segregation and at the same time be too close to Malcolm X's vision of Black Nationalism. If King's model of community was integrationist, Malcolm X's was separatist. Malcolm argued that an integrationist Christian approach was at its core accommodating to the dominant culture and would lead Black people to ape the ways of White people. Speaking from the perspective of the Black Muslims, Malcolm X argued that the Christian God advocated by King was partial in relation to White people.[6] How else would one explain the imbalance of economic and social power that White people controlled?

King's passion was the emergence of the Beloved Community, a community in which race, class, gender, and social achievements would give way to one's divine origin as that of being made in the image of God. It was King's dream that all who were in solidarity with the cause of Black people for basic human rights, equality, and dignity in this land would seek to make the dream of the Beloved Community a reality, "not through violence; nor through hate; no, not even through boycotts; but through love....But we must remember as we boycott that a boycott is not an end in itself...the end is reconciliation; the end is redemption; the end is the creation of the beloved community."[7] King was insistent that if oppressed people could claim divine resources in the quest to create the Beloved Community, they would defeat the evils of racism, classism, and materialism. King argued that the victory in Montgomery was not made possible because of creative leadership or the fact that Black people had grown tired of racism, but because the personal God at the center of the universe worked with them. The confidence that the personal God at the center of the universe works with the oppressed renews their commitment to community.

Something New: Beyond Black and White

Throughout most of his life, King was not concerned, primarily, with a commitment to the Black community; he felt that this could be construed as a way to keep segregation in place or to posit a reversal of roles. To proffer the replacement of White community with Black community would only change the color of the participants, but the same values would be at play. Instead of White supremacy there would be Black supremacy. King was pressing for something new beyond Black and White, something new that included both Black and White persons but allowed for a new community to emerge. This new reality was what King called the Beloved Community. "We must all learn to live together as brothers, or we will all perish as fools. We are tied together in a single garment of destiny, caught in an inescapable network of mutuality. And whatever affects one directly affects all indirectly....This is the way God's universe is made; this is the way it is structured."[8]

Theologian King tells us of the length God would go to restore broken community. He observed that his understanding of the death of Christ on the cross was a signal and symbol of the distance God was willing to go to restore broken community. As a good Baptist pastor and theologian, King saw sin as a fractured relationship between brothers and sisters and between human beings and God. King found racism very repulsive not only because it was the sin of White people against Black people, but because it was, in the final analysis, sin against God. The cross then was the eternal symbol of

God's mission to restore broken community. Resurrection becomes God's victory over the forces that seek to block and destroy community and the Holy Spirit is the continuing force throughout history that makes community possible. There was no higher vocation for human beings than to join in the creation of authentic community. Wherever genuine community emerges, the rights of those on the margins of society will be taken seriously. Social justice is always the result of authentic community. Basic human rights for those on the margins are a theological and moral baseline for authentic community.

King's understanding of human community is replete with insights for the practice of pedagogy. Of first importance for him was the sacredness of each person. Every human being by virtue of being human has inherent worth and no person, society, or culture has any right to deny his/her personhood. Therefore, "to be free is to be human and to be human is to be free." It is here that King speaks of sin as anything that violates community, humanity, and one's personal freedom. The absence of freedom is the negation of personhood. Persons must be able to be responsible and have the opportunity to make decisions as they move toward freedom. To be unable to choose where one will go to school, where one will live, or how one will survive is to compromise one's humanity. To deny one's basic human right to life, freedom, and justice on the basis of race, gender, or class is to take away that person's capacity to be responsible, to decide, to deliberate.

Historically, from the plantations in the South to the ghettoes in the North, Black people have been voiceless and powerless. They have been unable to make decisions that alter the structure of their lives. They have not had the power to affect the way they live. The absence of power to be responsible means that they may not be held responsible for their crimes, because their crimes have been derivative. They lack the power to change a system that crushes them. Speaking of the loss of power that is emblematic of the Black community King writes:

> The plantation and the ghetto were created by those who had power, both to confine those who had no power and to perpetuate their powerlessness. The problem of transforming the ghetto, therefore, is a problem of power confrontation of the forces of power demanding change and the forces of power dedicated to preserving the status quo. Now power properly understood is nothing but the ability to achieve purpose. It is the strength required to bring about social, political and economic change.[9]

Love provided a moral horizon for power and an openness for Black people to reject segregation. King's passion against segregation was because he was convinced that it was a threat to an inclusive community. In many of King's speeches was the refrain "I cannot be all that I ought to be until you are all that you ought to be and you cannot be what you ought to be until I am what I ought to be."[10] For King, community at its best depended on the interrelatedness and mutuality of persons. It was clear for King that unless we learned to live together as brothers and sisters we would all perish.

However, King was not insulated from the darts of racism. Growing up in Atlanta in the 1940s he would pass places where Black people were lynched and would see the Ku Klux Klan on its nightly ride to harass Black people. Although he grew up middle class, this did not protect him from racist insults and humiliation. Yet, it was in the context of the Black church that he experienced the healing balm of community. It was in the Black community, which called him to serve after his matriculation from Boston University, where an ethic of care made a difference to him and he experienced love conjoined with power in the practice of love toward self. Somehow in this community, sustained by a common faith and threatened by a common fate, the community reached beyond itself and offered healing and respite to weary travelers.

Living in the Tension between Black and Beloved Communities

Perhaps, in the end, it was because of the pervasiveness of Black faith and the healing provided by the Black community in a racist environment that King began to sound more like Malcolm X when he instructed the Black community to affirm Black institutions. One may argue that the early King of the 1950s and mid-1960s leaned toward the promise of the American dream becoming a reality in his own time. His sense of community that would serve as a creative context for human flourishing was one that existed beyond Blackness and Whiteness. But it seems that certainly after 1966, King began to reevaluate the dream and began to conclude with Malcolm X that the possibility of his dream for America morphing into a nightmare was not far fetched. He was surprised at the intransigence of racism and as his "Letter from a Birmingham Jail" made clear, he had lost confidence in the courage of the White middle class to help effect social change on behalf of oppressed people. He began to instruct oppressed Black people to develop self-reliance and a commitment to create their own businesses. And a part of what it meant to develop Black business was a readiness to withdraw economic support from Coca Cola, Sealtest milk and Wonder Bread, which he claimed were not committed to treat all God's children fairly.[11]

It seems that for King the goal was still the Beloved Community, where Black people and White people share power and work toward economic justice. But King raises an important question: What if the Beloved Community becomes a mirage? What if the vulnerable are being exploited by people with power even in what appears to be an embryonic form of this community? The challenge says King is to embrace economic power within one's indigenous community. Black people must negotiate from the perspective of power.

> We've got to strengthen black institutions. I call upon you to take your money out of the banks downtown and deposit your money in Tri-State bank—we want a "bank-in" movement in Memphis.... You have six or seven black insurance companies in Memphis. Take out your insurance there.[12]

For genuine community to emerge we must abolish the inferior and superior hierarchy extant in many communities. "We are called to speak for the weak, for the voiceless, for the victims of our nation, and for those it calls enemy, for no document from human hands can make these humans any less our brothers."[13]

It is quite clear that King understood segregation as threat to the integrity of the Beloved Community. Segregation as a threat pre-empted the promise of integration in which Black people and White people could come together to study, learn, teach, work, and play. King was committed to this articulation of the American dream in which people in spite of the color of their skin would be celebrated because they are children of God. For King, segregation also affirmed the racist structure of society that rendered Black people as inferior and Whites superior. And in educational settings this was played out in terms of unequal opportunities and resources. Of course the inequity of resources continues to plague education today because of the imbalance of financial and human capital. It still is the case where we have all-Black colleges where their resources in terms of libraries, scholarships for students, and salaries for staff and faculty are well below the average in White institutions. This, certainly as King saw it, was one of the problems with integration: the imbalance of power in terms of economic resources and human capital.

King was convinced that the challenge facing America as it confronted segregation in education and in other arenas of social and cultural life was to find a Christian perspective in race relations. Can the Christian faith provide Black community with a framework of meaning that honors the Black experience? This was the challenge that faced King as he proffered integration as the way forward as a response to segregation and Jim Crowism. The integrated community was not the Black community or the White community, but the American community. The bottom line was that King wanted to find a creative context in which his understanding of the Christian community could be played out. Although King did not want to destroy the American way of life he was clear that it was not consonant with the imperatives of the Christian gospel. An inclusive community was not just a question of social ethics, it was a mandate of the gospel of Christ. King was hopeful that the American dream would as closely as possible approximate his vision of Christian community.

Of course what King had not bargained on was the fierce resistance from the dominant culture and race to his project of integration. Black bodies were prevented from being present in classrooms, public accommodations, and hospitals. The Black body became the site of the fears, anxieties, and frustrations of White people. King was reminded by students that during the period of American slavery, Black people did not own their bodies. Because they were property the master had the legal right to whip, lynch, and treat Black bodies with impunity. The aristocracy often used lynching as a means of psychosocial, economic, and political control. The dominant culture regarded Black bodies as ugly and important only as a tool of labor. The Black body became the site of the struggle between bondage and freedom.[14]

> The schools of the south are the present storm center. Here the forces that stand for the best in our national life have been tragically ineffectual. A year after the Supreme Court had declared school segregation unconstitutional, it handed down a decree outlining the details by which integration should proceed "with all deliberate speed.".... But the forces of good will failed to come through. The Office of the President was appallingly silent, though just an occasional word from this powerful source...might have saved the South from much of its present confusion and terror.[15]

King did not anticipate such stubborn resistance to Black bodies hence his marshaling Biblical and theological arguments for integration. The first problem with desegregation of schools was getting the dominant culture to allow Black bodies to be present. They had to come to grips with the reality that it is Black bodies that study, write term papers, teach, and play. Especially in the American South where White people were accustomed to Black people as field hands or as nannies for their children it was not automatic for them to make the conscious move and see Black people as equals in a classroom setting. Although King was an apostle of nonviolence there were times when he had to rely on police force and at times on the National Guard for protection of Black people—Black bodies—either to protest peacefully or to gain admission to universities in the American South.

In more recent times, when there is an accommodation by the dominant culture to experiment with integration in educational institutions, the critical question concerns whether or not Black people have the power to be themselves. Critics of King on this question of integration, especially Malcolm X, have always raised the question as to whether integration means the loss of self for the Black person. Does integration mean that Black people sacrifice self, their voice? Does integration mean that as Black people change the dynamics of the classroom with Black bodies, they sacrifice self in a willingness to embrace White culture and thereby ape White ways of being and knowing? How much should the Black person be willing to give up, and yet remain true to her/his best self? It is worth remembering that Black theologians warn us that sin is the loss of identity. Sin is separation from self and community.

A look at the curriculum of many colleges may suggest that the communities of Africa and the struggles of people of color are sacrificed in the instruction offered. King's comment in his American dream speech that people should be judged by the content of their character and not by the color of their skin may be construed in this sense and used against Black people. It could be construed as an attempt to sacrifice self. How may we talk about character, or education without talk about Black bodies?

King's attempt to provide a Christian frame of reference for liberation pedagogy raises the question as we move from segregated classrooms to integrated ones: "Are Black bodies welcome?" An index of this question has to do with texts that are chosen for the class, especially in the humanities. Are the texts able to help students make sense of their identity? Are Black students able to see themselves in terms of their history and culture as centers of value? For many of us who were taught to value Eurocentric authors and texts, it is a constant challenge to get us to value Afrocentric texts. Even for many of us who teach in all Black settings this critique remains true. We have to make an effort as teachers to recognize that part of what it means to love our students and to love the subject matter is to help students connect texts with their reality. We must help students see themselves in the texts. This is certainly the case with national tests that Black students are required to take. King taught us that we must connect the words we teach to the worlds of our students.

The other challenge that comes from the move from segregated to integrated classrooms is to what extent as teachers are we willing to create rhetorical space for marginalized students and those in the classroom who are most vulnerable to feel comfortable enough to risk being heard. The hierarchical space in many classrooms seems to suggest that the teacher is the only person who has a right to be heard. How may the teacher use this power to change the dynamics of the classroom? If we apply the principles that King taught concerning the right of oppressed people to justice, we may begin to talk about the teacher being willing to fight for justice on behalf of marginalized students. What does it mean for the creation of rhetorical space for all members of the class, especially those who are most vulnerable to feel that they belong and have a right to be heard? An important part of what it means to teach is to embrace the courage to be there in the classroom for those who are most vulnerable. How far are we willing to go as we stand in the gap for our students? What should genuine community look like?

Being There in Community for Each Other

If we were to isolate and identify a hermeneutical key for King as it relates to pedagogy it would be the aphorism: "I cannot be all that I can be until you are all that you can be, and you cannot be all that you can be until I am all that I can be." This was a test that King would apply to the sociopolitical situation, and it provided part of his confidence in the Beloved Community. This key provided an internal critique of how things were going in the community, whether all persons were being valued, and at the same time taking responsibility for the well-being of the community. This was another way of saying that we need each other and that the old order of oppressor/oppressed was inadequate for the wholeness of integrity and identity to emerge. King wanted to move beyond Black and White and assert that "we are caught in an inescapable network of mutuality."

Nevertheless, it seems that in spite of the press for integration and the commitment to the Beloved Community, because of his hermeneutical key that each of us needs to be his/her best self if community is to flourish, King seems to argue for a modified form of segregation in his counseling the Black community to place their money in banks owned by Black people, and not to patronize companies that were not pro-Black. Coupled with this was the reality that he never counseled Black congregations to integrate. The majority of Black churches have been segregated, both culturally and economically. The Black church has been one of the few institutions that is Black owned. Historically, this has been one of the few places where Black bodies have been free to study, teach, dance, pray, and learn. Also, it should be remembered that King, like both mother and father, attended segregated colleges. As King began to embrace Blackness, did he imply that perhaps there is a place for segregated schools after all, if this is the only rhetorical space where Black people are free to engage critical consciousness?

Could it be that in 1968, the year King was assassinated, he had come to see that although the Beloved Community had become the grand vision of the Civil Rights Movement, because of the depth of the racist worldview that informed and dominated America, he posited a limited form of segregation as an emergency situation? Could it be that King had finally come to understand the enormity of the problem of racism in America? He referred to racism as "the Black man's burden and the White man's shame." "It is an unhappy truth that racism is a way of life for the vast majority of white Americans, spoken or unspoken, acknowledged and denied, subtle and sometimes not so subtle—the disease of racism permeates and poisons the whole body politic. And I can see nothing more urgent than for America to work passionately and unrelentingly—to get rid of the disease of racism."[16]

The implications for the classroom and church are very clear. In this address King referred to Sunday mornings at 11 o'clock as the most racist hour in America when most White Christians worship their God in an exclusionary environment and many Black Christians worship in their own context. Teaching must face racism head on. That is, as King said, we must be aware in the classroom that whether spoken or not, acknowledged or denied many of the assumptions that inform pedagogy in the United States and certainly in contexts in which Euro-American worldview predominates, the tendency to elevate the Euro text or perspective is always very present. His instruction in his last sermon on April 3, 1968 to the congregation in Memphis, Tennessee is most appropriate to those of us who seek to relate community and pedagogy: "God sent us here, to say to you that you're not treating his children right. And we've come by here to ask you to make the first item on your agenda—fair treatment, where God's children are concerned. Now, if you are not prepared to do that, we do have an agenda that we must follow. And our agenda calls for withdrawing economic support from you."[17] The call went out to boycott businesses that were not treating God's children fair. I wonder what this would look like in the classroom and in an ecclesial context. What do you suppose it would mean to treat God's children fair in the classroom? King reminds us that a place to start is to welcome Black bodies, and to remember that it is bodies that study, learn, teach, work, and play.

But King not only admonished the congregation in his last words to boycott companies that were not committed to the flourishing of all of God's children but also pointed out that the time had come for the Black community to be proactive in building Black institutions. It is evident that the marching orders from King to the community were clear. The community must tackle the stubborn reality of racism. All God's children must receive fair treatment. It may include nonviolent direct action. But even further, Black institutions must be strengthened.

Theology of Black Power

The Student Non Violent Coordinating Committee (SNCC) had complained to Martin Luther King some years earlier that Black people were tired of being powerless and that the time had come to conjoin love with power, hence the cry Black Power. Because the year after King's death James Cone published his path-finding book *Black Theology and Black Power*, I would like to turn now to Black theology as a theoretical tool for pedagogy and see what we may discover in its attempt to create rhetorical space for Black people in the classroom. The first thing that must be stated in this new theology is that it was a celebration of Blackness, there was no attempt to distance itself from Black bodies. Black theologians felt that to cultivate disdain for segregation was in fact to cultivate disdain for the Black community. While Black theologians shared King's dream of the Beloved Community they did not place the emphasis there but in the exercise of power in the Black community. This means that the first order of business was accepting self, not negating self or advocating the denial or loss of self. It is clear that Black theologians regarded King as mentor and one who had laid out an agenda for them.

However, the Beloved Community was seen as an eschatological possibility, that which would happen in God's time perhaps at the end of history. In the meantime they set themselves the task of constructing a theology of the Black religious experience. This means that Blackness is not to be avoided or relegated to the realm of unimportance but that it is to be embraced and must become the point of departure for talk about God, self-worth, and humanity. James Cone's *Black Theology and Black Power* was the first text in liberation theology to insist that the loss of Black identity was sin against God and community. As we seek the implications of this theology for pedagogy we may begin to inquire about the shape of liberation pedagogy.

Cone asserts and affirms that we must begin with people. Theology in a racist context must not reduce people to abstractions, but must take them seriously in terms of their color. We must begin with Black bodies that learn, study, teach, and play and we must begin to inquire whether Black students have the resources and the cultural and social capital to do their best work. King suggested earlier that racism is the most urgent problem facing the United States of America, and James Cone took him seriously. Cone raises the question for us as to whether the deprecation of segregation is not in theory, if not in practice, an expression of self-hate. With this in mind and its implication for the practice of education, Black theologians and an array of other thinkers in the Black community posit the Black experience as the point of departure for reflection about self-worth and whatever concerns us at the fundamental levels.

This emphasis on the Black experience gives value to color, to Black points of views, and begins to create rhetorical space for Black stories and Black ways of being in the world. This emphasis on the Black experience refuses to value self only in the light of other selves that may be outside the Black community, but places emphasis on intra-community concerns. This, I believe, could be construed as one of the fundamental flaws of King's insistence of a community of selves that reside outside the Black community as a frame of reference for the human flourishing of Black people. King's insistence that there is this mutuality of being, this interdependence of being that is crucial for Black well-being raises the specter and allows the possibility of other communities holding Black people hostage. It seems to me that implied in Cone's position, especially when he embraces Black sources for the articulation of his worldview, is the notion that the Black community gathered to study, teach, play, or worship may be the only place or space where they may be assured of their somebodiness. The Black frame of reference becomes the only space where the promise of Black existence flourishing outweighs the threat of self-hate and rejection by the other.

This was the danger the students addressed to King that the imperative to love the other who was committed to destroy Black reality was an invitation to self-destruct. Black people admonished King to give precedence to their own social and cultural capital. They were called to build a community that did not define itself in relation to the other that was committed to destroy it, but to affirm self-worth and see the gathering of Black bodies as a place where Black somebodiness is celebrated. This means that color, the color Blackness, becomes an important key in identifying Black reality. This was a radical way of talking about Black reality: that of affirming that which has been the badge of inferiority, slavery, and bondage. For over two hundred years, to be born Black in the New World meant from the perspective of the people in power that you were born for bondage. To be born White meant that you were born for freedom. No wonder then that many thinkers and leaders in the Black community, among them the King of the 1950s to mid-1960s, observed that Black people could not be their best selves without White people. The truth is that many Black people still believe that and this thesis has disastrous consequences for liberation pedagogy. This explains why King was not at peace with segregation because for him segregation meant Black people could not provide social, economic, and social capital to be their best selves. The irony is that although King posited an oppositional theory that White people could not be their best selves without Black people, there were no White people who believed that.

An examination of White institutions bears out my observation. This was true of educational institutions where Blacks were bused across town amidst the protest of White citizens and in many institutions where Whites did not protest, they made sure that there were only token Blacks whose power to effect change was circumscribed. Blacks were forced to create Black caucuses and departments of African American Studies in which they could find Black sacred space for being and knowing. It is interesting that most of these departments of African American Studies, and certainly in the institution where I teach, the program of Black Church Studies, have one or two White students. White students do not buy the myth that Black people and White people "are caught in an inescapable network of mutuality and whatever affects one affects the other." While they may see this as an attempt to talk about the idealized self, they do not have to buy the myth that White people need Black people because they have the power to affect and effect change without Black people. They learned a long time ago that they can find somebodiness, White "somebodiness" in the American way of life. At the university where I teach in the American South, neither Black students nor faculty protest that most of the pictures, photographs that adorn the buildings are White. We accept it that White people need this for their flourishing. They need to see themselves in their art. But what does it mean for Black and other minority communities? In what sense does art mirror community? Are other communities allowed to see themselves in this mirror? It means that we have to find symbols and images that are affirming outside of White structures. This calls into question an integrated setting in which texts, culture, symbols, and images are an expression of White supremacy. How can pedagogy be liberating for Black people in such a setting?

Pedagogy and the Black Experience

It is precisely at this stage that teachers and students are encouraged and admonished by Black theologians to have the courage to talk about color and the importance of linking pedagogy to the Black experience. It seems to me that what happened with King's asking the Black community to declare an emergency situation in which the Black reality/experience provides the center of value for being and acting is an insistence that we have to live with double warrants as we seek to move forward in community and classroom. King was deeply moved in what had transpired in Memphis, Tennessee, with Black sanitation workers who were being victimized by the dominant culture. They were deemed to be at the bottom of the social and economic ladder and consequently to be unimportant. These Black sanitation workers were a metaphor for the situation in which Black Americans found themselves as being among the most vulnerable in society.

Because King had come to understand White supremacy and Black inferiority as the root cause of "original sin" in America, he recognized that the Beloved Community that he proffered was a part of the idealized self of which he dreamed. King did not give up on the Beloved Community, but he began to see clearly that in a racist context the Black experience was the door to the idealized self. His call for Black people to pool resources and to unify as a people was not an attempt to bury the Beloved Community, but it was a way of asking: What does it say about us as community when the most vulnerable among us are allowed to be the point of departure for reflection and praxis of communities of reconciliation?

King, in the light of the crisis that ultimately took his life on April 4, 1968, posited a new center for talk about restored community, the center was no longer an integrated self/community, but the Black experience as the center of a conceptual framework. Since King was a systematic theologian by training, it is appropriate to suggest that this may be an attempt to talk about the cross and resurrection in the framework of the Beloved Community. King's attempt to decenter the idealized self and place emphasis on the existential self as a point of departure is another way of talking about cross and resurrection. King saw the Beloved Community as the restored and redeemed community that had overcome racism and its varied forms of oppression. The Beloved Community was to emerge out of the ashes of racism and would lay to rest segregated existence in the United States of America. The suffering that was engendered by the Civil Rights Movement, persons being killed by lynch mobs and overzealous police, hundreds being imprisoned, and in the end, even the leader being assassinated was the price of redemptive suffering that was a prerequisite for the resurrected form of the Beloved Community.

What the strike by the sanitation workers in Memphis helped King to see was that his dream of the Beloved Community was the dream of the idealized self. It was the dream of the resurrected and restored community. While King could not give up the dream of resurrection, he had to confront the reality of the cross, not just as an event that happened two thousand years ago when Jesus Christ was crucified, but as a necessary part of the American experience. The cross has always been at the very heart of the Black experience in the United States. The cross is the symbol of suffering, and for Black America this suffering began when Black people were captured in Africa by mercenaries and shipped across the Atlantic Ocean like sardines to the New World.

Lerone Bennett, Jr. captures the grotesque that comprises the Black experience:

> The slave trade was not a statistic, however astronomical. The slave trade was people living, lying, stealing, murdering and dying. The slave

trade was a black man who stepped out of his hut for a breath of fresh air and ended up, ten months later, in Georgia with bruises on his back and a brand on his chest. The slave trade was a black mother suffocating her new born baby because she didn't want him to grow up a slave.... The slave trade was a pious captain holding prayer services twice a day on his ship and writing later the famous hymn, "How Sweet the Name of Jesus Sounds."[18]

King saw clearly that the cross as Black experience had to be embraced. This was not the time to flee the cross because one could not get to the Beloved Community except through the door of the cross. The tragic and the grotesque in the community must be embraced. In order to know the idealized self one has to come through the door of the cross. This places the Black religious experience at the center of a conceptual framework.

This is exactly what Black theologians in the first two decades of Black theology sought to do. Although the primary data for talk about the world, God, and humanity is the Black experience, they had an eye on the idealized self/community. They were not saying that for Black people to affirm self-worth and dignity they needed gifts of respect and kindness from White people. They felt that dignity and respect were their rights and they were demanding these virtues because they were coupling Black theology with Black power. Listen to the language of demand:

> Some preachers, like the Rev. Highland Garnet, even urged outright rebellion against the evils of white power. He knew that appeals to "love" or "goodwill" would have little effects on minds warped by their own high estimation of themselves. Therefore, he taught that the spirit of liberty is a gift from God, and God thus endows the slave with the zeal to break the chains of liberty.[19]

Black theology points to Blackness (cross) as the Black community's way of being in a hostile world that seeks to strip Black people of their dignity and sanctity. The attempt to appeal to love, reconciliation, or Beloved Community too quickly is an attempt to bypass the cross, the grotesque, and get to resurrection without having dealt with the cross. This is the problem that faces us in American society; we want a democratic state in which minorities do not have equal rights with White people. Democracy means equal rights, a willingness to allow the most vulnerable among us to have their vote, to have their rights. The lines are drawn for the articulation of liberation pedagogy. The most vulnerable among us must not be ignored; neither must they be caught up in the configuration of the whole. The most vulnerable among us must not be allowed to become lost in the larger community, and one way in which this happens is to talk about universals, the idealized self, or the Beloved Community. The attempt to suggest that the cross is the door to any meaningful discussion of the Beloved Community is to suggest that liberation pedagogy places the least among us, the foreigner, the stranger, those whose voice have been silenced because of being of the same race, gender, sexual orientation, or religion must be the way in to praxis and discourse about the contours of a liberated community.

Black theologian J. Deotis Roberts touches on the importance of the cross being an indispensable ingredient in talk about liberated humanity. He puts it this way:

> The Black Christian knows that grace is never cheap. When I was a boy, I used to hear older blacks sing in the black church: "I wonder what makes this race so hard to run?" Those Christians knew the meaning of suffering. They knew that grace is never cheap. Blacks know what it means to suffer with Christ and to share his agony....The rejection and shame of the crucifixion...is integral to the Black experience. When I was a boy I used to hear older people give the gruesome details of lynchings that took place in our Southern town in the presence of horrified blacks. They knew the meaning of cross-bearing. As an adult, I too have known in my own experience what it means to endure harsh treatment and unmerited suffering in black skin in a racist society. In the midst of these experiences, the cross has been to me a healing cross.[20]

I am grateful to J. Deotis Roberts for sharing his personal experience in his text on Black theology in which we are reminded that for many in the Black community the Christian race is hard to run. Some songs in the Black church remind us the way is strewn with prickles and thorns. When you are forced to live out your faith in a segregated church and have to struggle with the cross of racism and poverty that is extremely heavy, the Christian race is a hard race to run. But like Jesus before them, they run the race, carry the cross, and sometimes fall with it.

Struggling with Blackness and the pain it engenders is a very heavy cross. Roberts reminds us that what makes the cross our cross is because it is the cross of Christ, and this points to the depths of our suffering in that our suffering is divine suffering. According to

Roberts, Black people did not choose their suffering that is engendered by the cross of Blackness. In a profound sense, this suffering chose us and in that sense it is divine suffering, it is the suffering of Christ. Without this connection of the cross with the cross of Christ, Good Friday becomes a Bad Friday. It is rather strange that the people of the cross called Christians worship a crucified Christ. In Isaiah 53:2, this Christ possessed no form or comeliness. Black church people identify with this Christ who has made the Black condition his own. It is this inseparability between the Black community and Christ that allows Black people to sing, "Nobody knows de trouble I've had, Nobody knows but Jesus. Nobody knows de trouble I've had, Glory hallelu!" We sang this in the church in which I was reared as a child almost every Sunday and part of the reason we felt this was important for us was because the suffering was intense and often extreme, but we felt that Jesus who identified with our community knew and understood our suffering. Because Christ was in solidarity with the community, the cross was a "healing cross."

I am grateful to Roberts for the term "healing cross." According to him the embracing of the pain and suffering of the cross leads him to discover a cross that heals. This sounds like a contradiction of terms: a cross that heals. The initial reaction and retort is that the cross wounds. The cross has been rightly associated with misery, anguish, and death. After all, Jesus died on the cross. Again in the church in which I was raised we would sing:

> Dey crucified my Lord, An' He never said a mumblain' word
> Dey crucified my Lord,
> An' He never said a mumblain' word.
> Not a word, not a word, not a word.

The tragic and the grotesque are revealed in the cross. And as the Black community shares in the cross of Christ, it points to a divine dimension and depth in suffering. It is the solidarity of the community with Christ that makes the cross a healing cross as the community asks: "Who is this Jesus who knows all about our troubles? Who is this Jesus who sees all our troubles?" This Jesus is the essence of the suffering community, a community that struggles under the weight of the cross.

In a recent class at Emory University, I sought to share with my students this interesting insight of the Black experience providing a conceptual frame of reference for talk about God, world, and humanity.

I pointed out that the human experience was one in which there was a cross at the very center of our struggle to make sense of our time here on planet earth, and that in a profound sense the Black experience in the United States that points to the most vulnerable among us—in that Black people were stripped of their culture, and heritage, and language—provides the point of departure for talk about the contemporary cross at the very heart of what it means to be a Black person in this land. We observed in class that one of the differences between gayness and Blackness was that Blacks were born and usually socialized in a Black home, church, community, and often a segregated school, while gay persons were not socialized in similar fashion in gay culture. A gay student pointed out that he agreed that unless he shared with the class that he was gay it was not likely anyone would know. He observed that there was a sense in which he could hide his identity as a gay person while this was not an option for Black persons as Blackness was a public badge that revealed their identity.

This observation led the class to talk about Blackness in public space in which issues of the shame of slavery and racial segregation are there for everyone to examine. Another member of the class observed that the loss of language experienced among Black people in their sojourn in the New World sets the Black experience apart as the contemporary cross as the loss of language signaled the loss of identity for Black people in the United States. The class claimed that this is not true of other minority communities in the United States, which when their backs are against the wall may find identity in their culture. The class felt that his was an important way of talking about the cross at the very core of Black reality and that the uniqueness of this cross made it the cross of Christ that is at the same time indistinguishable from the communal cross. We were having an excellent discussion and embrace of the uniqueness of the cross of Christ that we believed to be indistinguishable from the essence of the Black community. We talked about the struggle with the cross of Blackness as the willingness to allow the most vulnerable, the least among us, those whose voice have been silent to be included. We wrestled with how to allow students who perceive themselves on the margin of the class to frame the discussion and give shape to the praxis that is necessary for engaged pedagogy.

If the cross becomes the door to liberation pedagogy, the door to emancipatory community, does this mean among other things that as community we struggle with the grotesque, with difference, and are willing to engage struggle with each other's pain? This was when one student pointed out that she felt like she was on the cross and did not find the cross of Christ or any cross for that matter a liberatory symbol. "I am black, gay and female" she said. "I feel like I have three strikes against me. I am thrice oppressed. I feel the weight of the cross and there is no healing in sight." I must confess at this point I wished J. Deotis Roberts was present to explain further how it was that he found healing in the cross of Blackness. Insights came to the fore as another student enquired if she felt alone, as if no one cared, or as if she were not accepted. She answered in the affirmative in both cases and expressed the wish that she was understood. It was here that she and the class began to discover that part of what it means to share in the cross of Christ is to enter into solidarity with others. The situation in which healing occurs is one in which we come to discover that as we stand with Christ we stand with others and that the love of Christ calls suffering and injustice into question. It is the presence of Christ among us as the suffering one who takes the community's suffering on himself and empowers the community to share in this communal cross that opens up a new future for us of healing and sharing and caring. It is this saving meaning of the cross expressed in a community that cares that Roberts alludes to as healing in the cross. The cross alienates as an individual seeks to bear it by herself but when she discovers that Christ is the essence of the community, she enters into solidarity with the community and discovers saving meaning at the heart of the cross.

Fear Making Room for Love

Professor Cone complexifies the problem for us in suggesting that one of the basic issues we have to face in building community is the reality of the fear factor. "Whites have a deep primordial and profound psychological fear of Blackness....Blacks fear whites too. But the Black fear of whites is often well grounded."[21] The major problem here is that people hate what they fear. "Many white policemen kill unarmed black people—shooting teenagers in the back—because they hate and fear blackness. One-third of black men we are told, between ages of 19–29 are involved in the legal system—i.e., in prison, on parole, or waiting for their case to come up in court....Approximately one half of the two million people in America's prisons are black. If such percentages were found in the white community, President Bush would declare a national emergency."[22]

The cross of Blackness causes Whites to fear Black people and it makes racial dialogue very difficult. Fear and hate are not helpful ingredients in building community. An important reality in the class-room context is that Whites and Blacks seldom get together outside the classroom. Cone observes at the New York seminary where he teaches, and I can attest to the same problem at the Atlanta University where I have taught for some thirty years, that outside of class, what we are likely to see in terms of Black/White relations among students are cliques of Blacks and Whites refusing to socialize along racial lines. Further, Cone suggests that the reality in the classroom is a spill over from the way we interact with each other in the society in which we live. The segregated patterns in our community take form in our classroom and certainly in our ecclesial communities. "Even in deseg-regated schools, workplaces and churches, self-segregation seems to be pervasive. Whites and people of color may be in the same schools, but they don't talk much to each other. Whites hang out with whites, blacks with blacks, Asians with their group and Latinos with theirs.... Why are we so content with living separate black, brown, red, and white lives?"[23]

It is clear that one reason for the fear of each other is the pain of separation. Except in a few isolated cases, Black and White people do not engage in practices of reconciliation. We are confident in our present status as separated people. We do not know each other and we fear what we do not know. It is important to note that according to Cone Black people also fear White people and there are two reasons, among others, for this Black fear that he claims is well grounded. Cone reminds us that the Black experience in America is one based on a long violent history of White supremacy. "There was little differ-ence between the white police in the South and North and the white hate groups like the Ku Klux Klan. The function of both was to terrorize blacks so that they would stay in their assigned place. Although white violence is more camouflaged and hidden today, it is just as real and brutal as it ever was."[24]

Another reason Blacks fear Whites is because they control their livelihood. If Black people step out of line they will find themselves looking for another job. White supremacy is omnipresent in the United States of America. "It is everywhere—controlling the centers of eco-nomic, political, intellectual and religious power. That is what white supremacy means—white control of all resources essential for human well being.... White institutions seldom change because a few token people of color are placed in high positions."[25]

It seems to me that Cone has gone a step further than Roberts to suggest that the cross at the heart of human existence in America defines both Black and White reality. The separation of the races engenders both fear and hate and an unwillingness to risk being human with each other. It is clear that the response of Black power is self-segregation and while this may spell pride of place and a sense of dignity among people who are helpless and hopeless in the face of White supremacy, it does not yet lead to a cross that heals or dialogue across racial lines.

The implications for learning and teaching are poignant. What are the signs of White supremacy in our classroom? Is the intellectual enterprise representative of White control? How are Blacks and other minorities represented in intellectual discourse? Are we afraid of dialogue across racial lines? How may we name this fear? Are there cases where fear leads to hate?

What May We Hope For?

Although Cone would not necessarily see the way forward as healing in the cross, his language closely approximates the reality to which Roberts points. Like Martin Luther King, Jr., he sees the goal as the Beloved Community, a community in which diverse groups may work for multiracial communities: communities in which people work together, worship together, socialize, and live together. The university should be proactive in advocating and working for the Beloved Community. This means the university, college, and seminary should acknowledge that there is a distance between where we are and our hopes and aspirations for community. "As religious people searching for racial reconciliation, we must begin the multi-racial dialog with repentance—profound recognition that we have all fallen short, that is as Christians say, sinned against God, our neighbors, and ourselves....The need for repentance is not just for whites but also for people of color. No one is without fault."[26]

According to Cone, people of color need to repent because of their failure to identify structural and systemic evil and their penchant toward passivity. People of color need to repent for the internalization of oppressive values and failure to take a stand for justice. On the other hand White people need to repent for the sin of pride, of thinking too highly of themselves. It is the self-criticism of repentance that sparks the possibility of change from a culture marked by fear of each other and the embrace of hate. Both White people and people of color need to be on guard for the capacity of the self to deceive itself. Although all are culpable for the fractures and fissures in community, those with the most power are most responsible. One of the goals of self-criticism in community is to redress the imbalance in power relations.

It is the critical question of how power functions in the community that makes Cone posit repatriation as the next step in building multi-racial communities. It is not enough in community building to say one is sorry. Black theology as it informs pedagogy insists that the move must be toward redressing the imbalance of power in the community. "Blacks, however, must not let whites off the hook on this issue. Demanding restitution is the only way that the oppressed can validate *their* repentance. Reparation is not welfare; it is justice."[27] We must ask: What would reparations as justice look like in the classroom? Would this be affirmative action or scholarships for Black students? However we decide it must affect the balance of power in the classroom so that Blacks do not suffer economically and politically.

The method of change as we seek to build community should be dialogue and there are three additional steps in building a community in which there is dialogue across racial lines. We should form small groups in which Black people would be comfortable and not intimidated by White privilege. It is in these small groups that we have the best hope of in-depth sharing aimed at changing the balance of power in community. Further, we must be willing to join in solidarity with each other with Whites being willing to transcend their existential circumstances. Cone concludes this article on the note of hope for better race relations reminding us that talk is cheap and we must do more than talk, we must be willing to take action, create a project around which we may all participate in which each of us has a stake. "Because multi-racial dialog is hard work, don't decide to enter into it because you want to help another racial group. Join because you want to help yourself. Join because you believe that what happens to one group happens to all."[28] Here, Cone explicates his theology of hope for a Beloved Community. But the hard question that we must answer is what may we do in the meantime between facing the real situation of Black powerlessness and the hope and aspirations for multiracial communities?

The history of race relations in America is one in which we know White people have no intention of doing an about turn and sharing power with people of color. The promise of forty acres and a mule for Black citizens was never honored. Therefore, to somehow believe that

White people are going to go along with a call for reparations, all aimed at restoring a balance of power in community is wishful thinking. It is clear that in Cone's call to form communities of dialogue and for action to take the place of talk about justice and power is indicative that the Cone of *Black Theology and Black Power* has moved from liberation to reconciliation. Has Professor Cone moved from his early passion made plain in his earliest text *Black Theology and Black Power* in which he joined with the Honorable Elijah Muhammad, Marcus Garvey, and Minister Farrakhan to question Black confidence in White supremacy? In reflection on Cone's first book, Professor Cornel West writes:

> Professor Cone raised a fundamental question that has pervaded the entire black freedom struggle: namely, whether there actually are enough intellectual, political and cultural resources in American life to fully undermine the vicious legacy of white supremacy in America. I discern in this text a death of faith in the promise of American democracy. I think that this particular sensibility is one that millions of people of African descent experienced after the death of Martin Luther King, Jr....What makes us think that America has the capacity to produce a full-fledged multiracial democracy in which people of African descent are treated as kindly and equally as anybody else in every sphere of our lives? What evidence do we have? Historically speaking, we have two hundred forty-four years of enslavement, seventy-one years of Jim and Jane Crow, fifty-one years of every two and a half days with some black child or woman or man hanging on some tree like the strange fruit that Billie Holiday sang about. What makes us think that just within these last twenty-five or thirty years, the significant progress and breakthrough made can cut deep enough so that these white supremacist sensibilities, be they subtly or not so subtly expressed, would not come back in the way they did after Reconstruction? What evidence do we have?[29]

It is clear that there is an epistemological shift in the thought of the early Cone of *Black Theology and Black Power* and his dream for a multiracial society. As he struggles with the evidence for his dream, in a version of American democracy he may need to reread his earlier text. The Cone of 1969 got it right; "... to ask blacks to act as if color does not exist, to be integrated into white society, is asking them to ignore both the history of white America and present realities....Instead, in order for the oppressed blacks to regain their identity, they must affirm the very characteristic which the oppressor ridicules—*blackness*.

Until white America is able to accept the beauty of blackness ('Black is beautiful, baby.'), there can be no peace, no integration in the higher sense. Black people must withdraw and form their own culture, their own way of life."[30]

Perhaps the way forward is to live in the tension between praxis aimed at changing the situation and the hope that White people will share power in such a way that the balance of power will be drastically altered in the classroom and in the culture at large. If history is any guide to the future, it seems to me that we must revert to a declaration of an emergency situation in which we do not lose hope for an eschatological in-breaking of the Beloved Community, but in the meantime we press for practical ways to increase the power of those who are marginalized and rendered mute in the classroom and society. Community has to be based on trust and with the history of oppression in the United States as our guide, it is dangerous to place trust in those who hold the levers of power. Cone hopes for too much from the stranger, from those who hold the levers of power. In the end King was disappointed and so are we.

2

What Can a Black Woman Teach Me?

As you may guess this is not my question as I have had Black women teachers over the years and I am willing to acknowledge that they have much to teach. But the question forces me, and I hope you, to reflect on the contexts in which you may have been open to Black women teachers. Perhaps because I was raised in a Black home, it was not unusual that I had Black women teachers in elementary and high schools. I recall two of my favorite teachers: Miss Campbell in first grade, who made me believe that I was bright and could be anything I dreamed of, and then there was Mrs. Taylor in third grade who allowed me to act the role of teacher in a school skit. The skit had such an effect on me that I have wanted to be a teacher ever since.

Yet, the higher up the academic ladder I climbed, the less I was exposed to Black women teachers. In the seminary context there was one Black woman teacher, a Methodist Deaconess, and many of us young theologues did not take her class. When I went off to Duke Divinity School in the 1970s and to Union Theological Seminary in New York also in the 1970s there were no Black women professors. I suspect these contexts were clear that Black women did not have anything to teach in these settings.

I also find it intriguing that in *Black Theology: A Documentary History, 1966–1979*, edited by James Cone and Gayraud Wilmore, a section on "Black Theology and Black Women" is in Chapter 5, almost at the end of the book, followed by a chapter on "Black Theology and the Third World," from which no Black theologians from Latin America or the Caribbean were asked to participate. In contrast, invited essays by White men were placed in the center of the book as Chapter 3. Editor Wilmore explains:

> Part V, we are willing to concede, is something of an embarrassment. Why should essays written by Black women be consigned to a separate section? The articles themselves, introduced by James Cone, who has experienced the burden of representing men before conferences of Black women theological students, defines the problem. Black theology has been a Black-male-dominated enterprise and to the extent that it continues to be so, our sisters say quite clearly, it cannot be an authentic means of liberation.
>
> The overwhelming predominance of Black women in our churches makes this situation all the more ironical. From the beginning of the movement women have been involved, but the very fact that we have gathered their contributions in one of the closing sections of the book is as much a testimony to institutional chauvinism as it is to their marginality.[1]

The question "What can Black women teach me?" is raised by womanist theologian Stacy Floyd-Thomas.[2] Wilmore acknowledges that in the Black theological enterprise Black men tend to speak for Black women. I believe that this may be one reason why even, unconsciously, James Cone introduces the section on "Black Theology and Black Women." It would have been very fitting to ask a Black woman to introduce that section but with the practice of speaking for women, it was natural for a male to introduce that section. As theology serves as source and resource for pedagogy, Black theologians and others must guard against speaking for Black women, and Wilmore counsels that when Black women speak we should not relegate their voices to the end of the text or marginalize their contributions as this practice will not serve as a means of authentic liberation.

With Black theologians marginalizing Black women, it is not surprising that womanist theologian Stacy Floyd-Thomas reports that when she enters the classroom as a scholar-teacher the question on the minds of her students is "What can a Black women teach me?" "In my academic context, when I enter the class room as a professor of Christian ethics and Black church studies, the first thing that many students engage is neither my mind nor my subject matter, but rather the fact that I am a black woman. My very embodiment creates dissonance for many students who (as I've been told) immediately ask themselves, 'What can a black woman teach me?'"[3]

As I invite womanist theologians to engage pedagogy, I would like in this chapter to look at three approaches to theology by womanist scholars with a view to identify and isolate their response to the question raised by Floyd-Thomas' students: "What can a Black woman teach me?" We begin with the contribution of Kelly Delaine Brown-Douglas, "Womanist Theology: What is its Relationship to Black Theology?"

Womanist Theology and Its Relationship to Black Theology

Womanist theology points to the richness of being Black and a woman in the United States of America. In a culture in which Black womanhood is devalued, womanist theology provides a context of resistance and protest to the multiforms of oppression that afflict Black women, while at the same time it symbolizes the affirmation of Black womanhood. "The use of the term womanist in religious and theological scholarship signals understandings of the Bible, various church communities, and God that have emerged from the social historical contexts of Black women struggling to survive and be free."[4] There are two tasks Brown-Douglas sets out to accomplish in her essay: 1) to point to the relationship she sees between Black and womanist theologies and 2) call attention to the points at which they converge and diverge.

Brown-Douglas reminds us that she began her theological studies as a student of James Cone with a central question: "Is the God of Jesus Christ for or against Black liberation?" Engaging Cone's *A Black Theology of Liberation* convinced her that God was on the side of the oppressed and that in a racist society such as the United States of America this confidence in the God who was on the side of the oppressed empowered her in the struggle against racism. Her journey toward womanist theology began with Black theology's struggle and engagement with racism and the ensuing conviction that in the United States of America, God and Christ were Black. "The image of a Black God gave me a new sense of pride in my own Blackness....But as I developed an awareness of what it meant to be a woman in a sexist society I saw the limitations of the Black God and the Black Christ."[5] If Black theology helped her to identify and deal with racism in church, academy and society feminist theology provided a critique of patriarchy within society and church as it helped her name the discrimination she experienced at the hands of Black men. "It was sexism. I became painfully aware that sexism was not just a 'White woman's thing.' It also pervaded the Black church and community. This meant that if the entire Black community was to be free, both racism and sexism, at the very least had to be eradicated."[6]

Brown-Douglas gets to the heart of the matter as she points out why we need to go beyond Black theology. At its core, Black theology was and is one-dimensional. It does an important job in taking on racism in American society and it does this in a powerful way in that it speaks out of the Black power and the civil rights milieu. But the problem with its analysis of White reality and Black existence is it neglected to incorporate the experience of Black women. She gets to the heart of the matter:

> Shaped by the Black power/civil rights movement out of which it emerged, Black theology focused only on one dimension of black oppression—White racism. Its failure to utilize black women's experience further prevented it from developing an adequate analysis of black oppression. It did not address the multiple social burdens, that is, racism, sexism, classism, and heterosexism, which beset Black men and women. Consequently, it presented an image of God and Christ that was impotent in the fight for Black freedom. A Black God could not empower Black women as they confronted sexism.[7]

We are led by Brown-Douglas to see both the limits and the possibilities of Black theology. Black theology helped provide the language for reflection and analysis of White supremacy in America, and it helped to empower the community in its fight against racism and its press for democracy in America, where Black people would be able to claim the equality and dignity that White America takes for granted. But the dilemma, says Brown-Douglas, was the rendering of Black women's experience invisible.

The resources marshaled in the fight against the monsters that were killing Black people were drawn only from the Black male community, and when there was a nod in the direction of the Black women they were relegated to back of the bus or to Chapter 5. This meant that the liberation project was limited to the eradication of racism and the evils of sexism, classism, and heterosexism were unattended. One wonders to what extent this myopic way of being reflected in Black theology's neglect of gender issues and classism is a carryover from the Black church's experience. It is widely acknowledged that in the majority of Black churches in the United States of America, women are not allowed or encouraged to share in leadership positions throughout the church. Many women never make it beyond being minister of music or an associate pastor. There are not many Black churches that call women as senior pastors. Although women comprise the majority of the church population, their responsibilities in terms of ministerial leadership is circumscribed. The question being raised is, to what extent the myopia exhibited in relation to Black theology's neglect of Black women's experience is a carryover of the Black church ethos?

This question is of first importance as Cone informs us in *A Black Theology of Liberation* that the church is the home of theology, and that it is not the task of the theologian to manufacture his/her own views of God and reality, but to represent the church. Of course, Cone would agree that as the theologian struggles with the church's text, the Bible, the theologian is enabled to offer leadership, and like an Old Testament prophet, to call both church and theology to its essential task. The point hinted at by Brown-Douglas is that Black theology as the theology of the Black church too closely approximates the ethos of the Black church and society. It is in this regard that womanist theology seeks to be prophetic as it points out that Black theology did not go far enough because the Black God it represented and offered was impotent to take on the complexity of Black existence and to help Black people fight for liberation in a complex world. "This God could not affirm or empower black women as they confronted sexism." As Brown-Douglas acknowledges the imbalance and injustice that has plagued women in church and society, she points out that while Black theology was interested primarily in tackling systemic racism in American society and church, it did not go far enough in exposing the evils of sexism.

However, because Black theology is foundational to womanist theology Brown-Douglas highlights for us from a womanist point of view some of the essential contributions of Black theology. Black theology provided for the Black community the language to talk about reality and God and to ask questions about the ordering of society. Black theology let it be known that God did speak through the Black community. The strident articulation of a Black God and Christ made clear that the Black story of suffering and struggle was God's story, and this was a story necessary to tell. Black theology opened the door for Black people to further explore the richness of their own experience in their efforts to understand the meaning of God's presence in human history. "Essentially, Black theology laid the groundwork for the emergence of various theological voices from the Black community, including womanist voices."[8]

The contribution of Black theology was enormous in validating the importance of Black people's experience as source and resource for the liberation project. What was ironic as implied by Brown-Douglas is that Black theology committed a similar sin against Black women that was perpetrated by White theologians against the Black community. The early Cone, in *A Black Theology of Liberation*, points out that the reason for Black theology coming into existence was because White religionists rendered the Black community invisible in the articulation of White theology. Black people were not represented. Cone observes in that early text that it is always important to ask who is excluded. And the Black community noted that Black people were excluded. It is interesting that in Karl Barth's multivolume *Church Dogmatics* I can only find one reference to Christianity in Africa, and it was his claim that there is no African Christianity.[9] With a similar logic, he would contend there is no Black or womanist theology.

Although Cone regards Barth as the most important non-Black source in the articulation of his theology, he does not posit the radical disjuncture to which Barth alludes between theology and culture. Unlike Barth, culture is an important source for Cone. This is one reason why it is surprising that in his articulation of Black theology he limited his critique and exposition to the African American male experience, all the time claiming that he was speaking for the total Black experience. "Womanist theology has emerged partly because of Black theology's failure to address the concerns of Black women."[10] Black women's experience was excluded and this was also true of the Black experience represented in the Black Diaspora.

Professor Brown-Douglas maintains that there are two distinctive themes to keep in mind as one relates Black theology to womanist theology. On the one hand is the insistence on the priority of the Black experience in the formulation of theological discourse and on the other hand is the exclusion of the Black woman's experience. According to Brown-Douglas: "While Black theology's starting point—the Black experience—does not include Black women's experience, womanist theology begins with Black women's story of struggle. Womanist theology reflects at least two aspects of that story: first, the complexity of Black women's oppression and second, Black women's resolute efforts to survive and be free from oppression."[11] Womanist theology wants to talk about Black women's struggles, both in the wider society and in the Black community, with the conviction that God participates in the struggle to defeat the multiforms of oppression that assail Black women. According to Brown-Douglas there is a push in womanist theology to identify and isolate the particularity of Black women's experience as the starting point for theological reflection. This as she observes is in contradistinction to Black theology, which purports to speak for the Black religious experience.

What is interesting as a methodological statement and replete with pedagogical insights is womanist scholars saying to Black theologians you do not speak for us. The same is true of Third World theologians who say to both womanist and Black theologians, you cannot speak for us. This is an important methodological premise, the tendency of communities and persons with power to choose to speak for those who are perceived to be powerless. To speak for another, seemingly to steal another's voice, is to perpetuate the cycle of oppression. I am often disappointed to see people with power make decisions and decide who is to be excluded and in so doing choose one of their members to speak for the poor and oppressed. This was one of the problems with the Black theological enterprise posturing that it represented the fullness of the Black experience and choosing who could speak for women and Third World people. The oppressed must speak for themselves and a form of discovery takes place as they coin their own words and name their own reality. In the process of discovery that takes place, they begin to realize that they make history; they begin to learn that they are teachers and students who can change the world. Coupled with the confidence of the oppressed that they can name their own reality and speak their own word is the faith that God supports them in their struggle to survive and to change the world.

The Problem of Double Jeopardy: Gender and Race

Kelly Brown-Douglas is emphatic that Black women's struggle for liberation should not be confused with that of White women as White women historically were a part of White privilege in contradistinction to Black women.

> The first distinctive women's liberation movement in America evolved out of abolitionism. These early feminists were struggling against what has become known as the Victorian idea of womanhood that undergirds patriarchy. This idea not only relegated White middle-class women to the domestic realm, but it also considered them fragile "dolls" who had to be placed upon a protective pedestal. As White

women fought for the right to vote, their concern for "women's rights" did not cross the barriers of race. They did not seem interested in the plight of their Black sisters. "The realities of slavery guaranteed...that Black women were never treated as White women were. Black women were overworked, flogged and otherwise exploited, just like men."[12]

As womanist theology sees itself in relationship to feminist theology, it insists that the racial bias in society must be distinguished from sexual bias. The womanist theologian has to deal with "the woman question and the race question." Historically, the Black woman has been interested in both and it is this twoness so to speak that allows womanist theology to both identify and differentiate itself from the White woman and the Black man. The Black woman is so to speak both insider and outsider. She is an outsider, who because of the reality of gender, is able to relate to the White woman and in her capacity as "Mammy" in White homes functions as insider. Because of her race she is an insider who functions within the context of her race and community, and she is often oppressed because of her gender.

Patricia Hill Collins in her important essay "Learning from the Outsider Within,"[13] argues that African American women have functioned as insiders in relation to White families for many years. "Countless numbers of black women have ridden buses to their white 'families,' where they not only cooked, cleaned, and executed other domestic duties, but where they also nurtured their 'other' children, shrewdly offered guidance to their employers, and frequently became honorary members of their white 'families.'"[14]

I became aware of this phenomenon several years ago at the university where I teach in the American South. I have had Black students who tell stories of their mothers being mammies to White children and in some cases suckling babies as surrogate mothers. On the other hand I have had White students, both male and female, confide that the only "real" mother they knew was the Black mammy. The critical point that both Black and White students make is that in spite of her insider status, the Black woman remained an "outsider within" because of her race. The Black woman is forced to see reality from within the tension of her racial and sexual identity and is often torn in either direction. She is forced to be bifocal, relating to both worlds and not being fully accepted in either.

Francis Beale captures the bifocality of the Black woman in her article, "Double Jeopardy: To Be Black and Female."[15] The problem, as she sees it, is that the Black woman finds herself in a unique situation in that although she is privy to the secrets of both the Black and White worlds, because she navigates existence in both gender and race, she experiences oppression in both.

> Unfortunately, there seems to be some confusion in the Movement today as to who has been oppressing whom. Since the advent of Black power, the Black male has exerted a more prominent leadership role in our struggle for justice in this country. He sees the system for what it really is for the most part, but where he rejects its values and mores on many issues, when it comes to women, he seems to take his guidance from the pages of Ladies Home Journal. Certain Black men are maintaining that they have been castrated by society, but the Black women somehow escaped this persecution and even contributed to this emasculation.[16]

Beale complexifies the issue for us as she suggests that the Black woman in the Black home "is the slave of the slave." The Black woman is often accused by the Black man of participating in his oppression.

> By reducing the Black man in America to such abject oppression, the Black woman had no protector and was used, and is still being used and in some cases, as the scapegoat for the evils that this horrendous system has perpetrated on Black men. Her physical image has been maliciously maligned; she has been sexually molested and abused by the white colonizer; she has suffered the worse kind of economic exploitation, having been forced to serve as the white woman's maid and wet nurse for white offspring while her own children were more often than not starving and neglected. It is the depth of degradation to be socially manipulated, physically raped, used to undermine your own household, and to be powerless to reverse this syndrome.[17]

Patricia Hill Collins warns about stereotyping the Black female experience, yet as Beale counsels, womanist thinking may not ignore the harsh circumstances that inform the lives of Black women. It seems that what all three scholars point to is the penchant for the Black woman to be treated as object at home, church, and work. To treat human beings as objects rather than subjects is to dehumanize persons, and one way out of this as Beale suggests is for Black women to seize the power of self-definition. It is very easy in a culture in which one is constantly and consistently demeaned to look to others for value and self-definition. Both Beale and Brown-Douglas suggests that in many ways Black women looked to the "other" to provide that sense of self, but in the case of the Black experience as resource for talk about Black humanity, women discovered that they were excluded. They were excluded because their own experience as woman was not a frame of reference for talk about Black reality. Black female survival demands that Black women seize the power of self-definition and speak and act from a womanist frame of reference being free to name their own reality as is referenced by Beale's claim of double jeopardy.

Womanist theology points to the interlocking reality of race, class, and gender in any attempt to talk about Black woman's reality. Brown-Douglas reminds us that the focus on class also calls attention to distinctions between Black and White women's experiences. "As White women, especially middle-class college women, 'gained experience in collective organizing' through their involvement in Black protests, and confronted gender discrimination within the civil rights movement, they were radicalized to fight for their rights within American society. This fight was characterized by the struggle against the same patriarchal order that had earlier deprived women of voting privileges. They demanded freedom from their exile in the domestic realm and access to the male-dominated social-political realm."[18]

According to Brown-Douglas, White woman's narrow focus on patriarchy made them disinterested in Black women's freedom struggles. The issue was different. Black women were concerned with survival issues, racial discrimination, and the Black family. On the other hand White women could not deny that in their quest to join White men in the private sector, Black women would be called on to take care of their children and run their homes. Further, Black women could not expect White women to become passionate in the fight against racism. There were Black women who wondered if the fight against patriarchy was an attempt to distract attention away from the fight on racism.

With these realities in mind, Black women joined the Black freedom struggle and sought liberation in that context. "What was Black women's status in the freedom struggle? Many of the African American women involved in this struggle soon discovered that the civil rights/Black power movement was as sexist as the women's movement was racist Although Black women helped found some of the freedom fighting organizations, spearheaded local protest activities, and risked their lives for the Black community's freedom, they were rarely afforded the opportunity to hold national leadership roles or have decision-making responsibilities within various organizations."[19] A more insidious problem was the equating of freedom from racism with the rights of men in their search for positions. Black women discovered early that they were not included in men's search for freedom. The problem, says Brown-Douglas, was that the paradigm being used by Black men was taken from White patriarchy. "Just as they [Black women] realized that their freedom was not a priority of the White-dominated women's movement, Black women discovered that they could not obtain their freedom through the male-dominated civil rights/Black Power movement."[20]

The Politics of Wholeness

As Black women began to relate to the women's movement and the freedom movement, the critical question for them was whether they were working for the liberation of the entire community, both men and women. "Black women were searching for a politics of 'wholeness.' They needed a political strategy that would insure Black people, men and women, rights to live as a whole, that is, free, human beings and that would keep the Black community whole, that is, unified, struggling together to survive and be free in relationships of mutuality."[21]

The implications for pedagogy and the study of Black theology are clear. Womanist theology as it engages pedagogy wants to focus on wholeness. In the language of Brown-Douglas it wants to focus on a sociopolitical analysis of "wholeness." That is, unlike Black theology, it exemplifies a stubborn refusal to see reality only through the lens of racism. Its commitment is to sociopolitical analysis that will confront racism, sexism, classism, and heterosexism as they impact the Black community. There will be safeguards to ensure that hostilities and divisions between men and women, poor and rich are not honored.

> Black people have oftentimes discriminated against one another based on each other's light or dark-skinned complexion. A social-political analysis of wholeness will confront this vestige of racism within the Black community just as it will confront the presence of gender, sexual or economic oppression within the community. Essentially, a social-political analysis of wholeness will help womanist theology make clear that the Black community is not free if any of its members are "unfree" because of their color, gender, sexual preference or economic condition.[22]

Womanist theology must reflect Black women's struggle for the liberation of the entire community that includes a willingness to remove obstacles to liberation. It is quite clear that one of the new insights that womanist theology brings to liberation pedagogy and to Black theology is its refusal to merely look for the enemy on the outside, or in the other.

Brown-Douglas's take on womanist theology is fiercely committed to the building of and safeguarding of the Black community. Like Black theology, she is willing to take on racism for its evils, but beyond that she wants also to look within. A careful reader of Black theology will note that there are occasions when the test of Blackness is administered as Black theologians ask Black persons to examine their commitment or lack of solidarity with the Black community. One is reminded of an often-overlooked comment of James Cone in his book *Black Theology and Black Power*

> It is to be expected that many white people will ask: "How can I, a *white* man, become black? My skin is white and there is nothing I can do." Being black in America has very little to do with skin color. To be black means that your heart, your soul, your mind, and your body are where the dispossessed are.... Therefore, being reconciled to God does not mean that one's skin is physically black. It essentially depends on the color of your heart, soul, and mind.... The real questions are: Where is your identity? Where is your being? Does it lie with the oppressed blacks or with the white oppressor?[23]

This shows up on the last page of Cone's first book and is not often considered in an analysis of an internal critique of the Black community. This ontological expression of Blackness holds the Black community accountable, as Cone points out that it is not enough to be physically Black. There has to be a commitment to liberation that spells solidarity with the least of these.

Brown-Douglas picks up on this theme in womanist theology and seems to make this central. It is fair to say that because the starting point she advocates is Black women's experience of survival, the issue of what holds community together and the importance of the internal critique is much more central than in Black theology. In a profound sense, womanist theology is free to focus on the internal critique because Black theology has focused on the external enemy: racism. But the point is well taken by womanist theology that the emphasis is the politics of wholeness, which means that it deals with racism, sexism, classism, and heterosexism as they impinge on the well-being of the Black community. The primary responsibility is the protection of the community and the enhancing of whatever contributes to its well-being.

Womanist theologians also point out another distinction from Black theology: their understanding of God. Because of the emphasis on the protection of the community and the focus on the internal life of the community, notions of God as judge within the community are preeminent. Womanist theologians are correct in pointing out that the primary emphasis of Black theologians is that God will deliver Black people from Pharaoh and his hosts. Womanist theology raises questions about God's covenant with the community and what it means to live according to both grace and law within the covenant.

Anthropology as a Point of Departure in Womanist Theology

Next we listen to womanist theologian Linda Thomas in her article, "Womanist Theology, Epistemology, and a New Anthropological Paradigm."[24] According to Thomas, womanist theology seeks to interrogate the social construction of Black womanhood in relation to the African American community, as it engages critical conversation with Black males with a view to the development of a theology that points to a community that is whole. At the very onset, Thomas is insistent that dialogue between women and men in the Black community is crucial in the construction of a womanist theology. She states the problem for us:

> Womanist theology engages the macro-structural and micro-structural issues that affect black women's lives and therefore, since it is a theology of complete inclusivity, the lives of all black people. The freedom of black women entails the freedom of all peoples, because womanist theology concerns notions of gender, race, class, heterosexism and ecology. Furthermore, it takes seriously the historical and current contributions of our African forebears and women in the African Diaspora today. It advances a bold leadership style that creates fresh discursive and practical paradigms and "talks back" to structures, white feminists, and black male theologians. Moreover, womanist theology asserts what black women's experiences mean in relation to God and creation and survival in the world.[25]

Thomas seems to broaden her approach to womanist theology in contrast to Brown-Douglas. While Brown-Douglas raises questions regarding womanist theology's relationship to Black theology and specifies the ways in which womanist theology functions as a liberation theology, making space for emancipatory praxis in the Black community, Thomas seems to broaden the scope as she is more intentional in including both Black history and culture as sources for the fashioning of this theology. "Womanist theology draws on sources that range from traditional church doctrines, African American literature, nineteenth-century black women leaders, poor and working-class black women in holiness churches, and African American women under slavery. In addition, other vital sources include the personal narratives of black women suffering domestic violence and psychological trauma ..."[26]

This is an important methodological note that Thomas highlights: the inclusion of working-class persons in the construction of the narratives that inform womanist theology. There is the tendency in Black and womanist theologies to use the history and culture of heroes, intellectuals, and saints as sources for the articulation of our theologies. But Thomas widens the lens as she puts us on notice that the narratives and stories of the entire Black community constitute sources for the articulation of a theology that spells liberation for the entire community. The challenges to Black theology and to liberation pedagogy are clear. We have noted that a number of womanist theologians, among them Jacqueline Grant and Kelly Brown-Douglas, take Black theology to task for claiming to speak for the entire Black community, and in claiming to use the experience of the community as source for the articulation of this theology excludes the experience of women as it builds a theology based on the Black religious experience of Black males. These womanist theologians pointed out that Black theology is flawed at two levels: 1) Its claims to represent the entire Black experience is inaccurate as Black women's experience was excluded and 2) In its passion to speak to a racist structure and challenge White supremacy in American society, it ignored, and in some cases, was complicit with a patriarchal worldview that was alive and well in church and society.

These truth claims led these womanist theologians to state categorically that to correct this egregious error, womanist theology would take as its starting point the experiences of women's struggle for freedom as their point of departure for theological reflection and action. Womanist theology forces Black theology to expand its understanding and depiction of the Black experience. Thomas challenges Black theologians to clarify whose experience qualifies as the Black experience. Her anthropological methodology is inclusive of the working poor and of women throughout the Third World. "Womanist theology, moreover, grasps the crucial connection between African American women and the plight, survival, and struggle of women of color throughout the world. Womanist theology intentionally pursues and engages cultural contexts of women who are part of the African Diaspora. To enhance the networking of women all over the globe, the methodology of anthropology, a key discipline within the social sciences, aids womanist theology in this engagement."[27] The press for womanist theology to be in conversation with women of color throughout the African Diaspora opens the door to the possibility of fruitful dialogue and raises questions of what it means to expand the range of the Black experience.

For example, African Americans live in the richest country in the history of the world. In this context, a poor family of four persons makes in the neighborhood of $20,000 per year. In many poor countries in Latin America and Africa a poor family of four may not make $1,000 per year. What would this dialogue mean for the articulation of womanist theology? Would the understanding of community change? This has been a fundamental problem with Black theology that wants to speak for the Third World, but has to acknowledge that it does not know the Third World and the Third World does not see issues of race or gender as the central problem. The central issue has to do with the distribution of resources, with issues as basic as mothers being able to provide clean water and milk for children who are famished. It is quite a challenge for womanist and Black theology to give more than lip service to people of color throughout the African Diaspora.

The implications for liberation pedagogy are also far reaching when an anthropological methodology is employed. It means among other things that people are taken seriously in terms of their social location. Liberation pedagogy has to acknowledge different learning styles and allow teaching practice to reflect this. Students are also empowered to teach out of their own contexts, and the class finds ways of affirming teaching/learning as the practice of liberation. It seems to me that one of the rich contributions of the anthropological method advocated by Thomas is it helps pedagogy clarify its aims and goals. What would it look like for pedagogy informed by womanist theology to specify teaching/learning as a liberation project? How may teaching/learning guard against "anthropological poverty?"

The anthropological method that Thomas suggests also highlights the importance of women's languages:

> Womanist theology takes seriously the importance of understanding the "languages" of black women. There are a variety of discourses deployed

by African American women based on their social location within the black community. Some black women are economically disadvantaged and suppressed by macro-structures in society. Other African American women are workers whose voices are ignored by the production needs of the capitalist world order…Womanist theology showcases the over-looked styles and contributions of all black women whether they are poor, and perhaps illiterate, or economically advantaged…[28]

One of the hopes of this anthropological methodology that Thomas presses is its ability to help theology and the practice of pedagogy focus on class distinction that beset intragroup talk. There is an often unspoken understanding in the African American community "that you do not air your dirty laundry in public." This means that when problems of an intragroup nature are identified, there should not be any public forum for the discussion of these issues.

For example, a couple Januarys ago, I was invited to a ministerial forum in Charleston, South Carolina, to address the clergy on the life and thought of Dr. Martin Luther King, Jr. At the end of the program an elderly gentleman approached me and congratulated me "for not airing King's dirty laundry in public." This I believe was one aspect of the problem members of the Black community had with Bill Cosby for suggesting in a public forum that Black parents need to be held accountable for young people who have gone astray. Some persons observed that this discussion should be had behind closed doors not in a public forum. Thomas' suggestion that attention should be given to different forms of discourse within the Black community raises the need for intragroup talk. Working-class, poor, and middle-class Blacks often do not communicate and do not know how to communicate across class lines. The problem of different languages is often identified across racial and ethnic lines, but seldom within the context of the Black community. Access to certain kinds of discourse have been ways in which the dominant culture has excluded Black and poor people. People in power often dictate the rules of the language game, and those who do not know the rules, and thereby break them, are marginalized. We see this often in the classroom as different classes seek to find common ground, or one form of discourse is privileged, thus rendering those outside that discourse mute.

The challenge to provide rhetorical space in which working class and so-called illiterate persons are at home in affirming their some-bodiness is quite a challenge. Perhaps this is one of "the dirty linens we need to hang in public." Thomas suggests that in the case of Black and feminist theologies there was a failure to communicate with Black women because of the different presuppositions each theology postulated. In the case of Black theology, there was failure to communicate with Black women because the primary concern of Black theology was communicating with the dominant structures in society concerning the evils of White supremacy.

> The point of departure for black theology is white racism. Since white supremacy is a structure that denies humanity to African American people, black liberation theology examines the gospel in relationship to the situation of black people in a society that discriminates on the basis of skin color. Within black theology, the exodus story is a hermeneutical device used to draw a parallel between the oppressed Israelites and the oppressed African American community. Consequently, the liberation of the Israelites represents symbolically God's freeing of black people. First-generation black (male) theologians did not understand the full dimension of liberation for the special oppression of black women: this was their shortcoming. To foster the visibility of African American women in black God-talk, womanist theology has emerged. Unlike black theology with its emphasis on race, feminist theology addresses the oppression of women, though primarily white women. The project of feminist theology did not deal with the categories of race and economics in the development of its theological discourse.[29]

In a profound way Black and feminist theologies did not create sacred space for dialogue with Black women because their starting points were radically different. Not only did Black theology concern itself with race in contradistinction to gender, thereby failing to address issues of sexuality and identity affecting Black women, but there was no basis for communication. Additionally, with sameness as a frame of reference, Black women belong to the same race, often the same religion and ethnicity Black men assumed they could speak for them. In Black culture, it was often seen as beneficial for the male to speak for the woman. The bottom line is that what was not helpful about the approach of Black theology was that the Black male experience was placed at the center of the conceptual frame of reference, thus marginalizing the Black female experience. In womanist theology, Black women broke their silence as they began to name their own reality.

It was also assumed that because both Black and White women share the same gender, Black women would understand themselves under the rubric of feminist theology. Thomas indicates that Black women were faced with a similar dilemma in relation to White women, who did not see issues of race and economics as an important frame of reference for talk about liberation. Black women found themselves excluded as their issues were not represented, and at its best, White women sought to speak for them. This certainly is one form of the double jeopardy that Black women have to face in their struggle for liberation. The tendency of both Black men and White women seeking to speak for them and in some instances being clear that they know what is best for them. Further, according to Thomas, Black women are uncomfortable with the penchant of feminist theology to position itself in opposition to men. "In a related fashion, too often white feminist theology creates a paradigm over against men; it is an oppositional theological discourse between females and males. In contrast, woman-ist theology recognizes patriarchal systems as problematic for the entire black community—women, men and children."[30]

While womanist theology appeals to the justice and judgment of God to challenge obstacles in the community that thwart human flourishing, their focus concerns the liberation of the entire commu-nity. There is no attempt to save women and condemn men, the goal of womanist theology is that both must be saved, but what is unique and different from Black theology is the insistence that it is only women who are able to marshal the resources of the community to save the entire community. The evil of patriarchy gets in the way and blinds men from seeing the ways in which they privilege their own experience, and thereby thwart the flourishing of the community. In a sense, the way womanist theology speaks of patriarchy in relation to men is to suggest that it is original sin. It is a privilege into which men are born irrespective of their race or social condition and it is a posi-tion that is reinforced by the church and the church's book, the Bible. In a patriarchal world women are identified from the perspective of men and are always regarded from a secondary and subordinate role. Patriarchy points to a context or worldview in which male privilege is based on the marginalization of women. Thomas reminds us that in this worldview that informs Black theology, and I daresay much class-room practice, the male is projected as the valued and the female as one who benefits from a relationship with the male. In a profound sense the male stands in for God. The male represents God.

It begins to become clear why Thomas and other womanist thinkers are insistent that at the core of womanist theology is women's experi-ence as the point of reflection for talk about what it means to be human and what it means to practice emancipatory pedagogy. A part of what womanist theologians are saying is that reality cannot remain the way it is constructed in the Black community, in church, and in society, because at the core of these ways of being is the notion of male supremacy, and not only are cultural arguments used to keep this worldview intact, but theological arguments are deduced. Christians often cite 1 Corinthians 11:3 "But I want you to understand that Christ is the head of every man, and the husband is the head of the wife, and God is the head of Christ." Or again in Ephesians 5:22–23, "Wives, be subject to your husbands as you are to the lord. For the husband is the head of the wife just as Christ is the head of the church, the body of which he is savior." These texts are often used to undergird the subordination and oppression of women. One way to begin to dismantle patriarchy is to posit a different point of departure. It is to begin with the most vulnerable among us, the Black woman, and to allow Black women ways of being in the world to provide the conceptual frame of reference for the way we navigate reality. It is to begin to ask what would the Black community look like if the point of departure for talk about who we are and what we desire to become is not some notion of man lording it over woman, but a new egalitarianism and democracy with women's ways of knowing and being as the entry point of constructing new knowledge about ourselves? Perhaps at his best St. Paul came close to this ideal of community when in 2 Cor. 5:17 he said "If any one is in Christ he/she is new, the old is past and lo all things are new." It is clear that for Paul being in Christ was his attempt to talk about a new social reality in which old ways of construing the world and reality were dated, and the challenge was to evidence new reality, new ways of being human in the world. I believe womanist theology holds out this possibility for us; those who for so long have been excluded take their rightful place in the community, and their language, new ways of being in the world, begin to shape reality differently.

For example, as womanist ways of thinking are related to pedagogy and the need to learn and teach in a way that fosters the practice of liberation, issues of diversity and inclusivity come to the fore. Giving voice to those who have been excluded and watching them move from the margins to the center in their construction of reality calls for new ways of relating in the academy, the church, and society.

Lesbian/Womanist Theology

In the final section of this chapter on the implications of womanist ways of knowing and being in our world, and what it means for learning and teaching, we listen to womanist scholar Renee L. Hill in her article: "Who Are We for Each Other? : Sexism, Sexuality and Womanist Theology."[31] Hill reminds us that womanist theology as it came on the scene sought to stand in the gap between Black theology, that highlighted the Black male experience as it resisted structural and personal racism, and White feminist ways of being, that sought to dismantle patriarchy. Both of these expressions of liberation theology sought to speak for Black women, but both failed miserably because they did not include the experiences of everyday Black women. As womanist theology addresses this void and omission, it seeks to speak and act from a place of resistance to the multiforms of oppression that are endemic to Black female existence. The place of resistance is Black women breaking the silence and refusing to be content to allow others to speak from their experience and claim that they are speaking for Black women.

While the conversation between womanist scholars with Black and feminist scholars has been helpful, Hill presses for an intracommunity conversation among womanist scholars and identifies a problem: "... Christian womanists have failed to recognize heterosexism and homophobia as points of oppression that need to be resisted if *all* Black women (straight, lesbian, and bisexual) are to have liberation and a sense of their own power. Some womanists have avoided the issue of sexuality and sexual orientation by being selective.... The tendency to be selective implies that it is possible to be selective about who deserves liberation and visibility."[32] Hill raises the importance of intracommunity discourse as she asks not merely who is not heard, but also who is rendered invisible not by Black males or White feminists, but by Christian womanist thinkers. Her answer is clear: Black women are excluding sisters with a different sexual orientation and this she claims is against the very meaning of "womanist" let alone Christian.

> Alice Walker's definition of womanism is about Black women shaping community. It is about Black women struggling and surviving. Walker's womanism is about Black women celebrating themselves and their communities. Her definition is also about relationships: relationships between Black women and the Black community; between Black mothers and their daughters.... Walker writes that a womanist is "a woman who loves other women, sexually and/nonsexually. Appreciates and prefers women's culture, women's emotional flexibility (values tears as natural counterbalance of laughter), and women's strength." The womanist is women oriented. She loves women. Womanism includes the woman's voice, the voice of Black women in relationship with each other.[33]

Hill makes a very bold claim that the voice of Black lesbian women is silenced not by those one might expect, but by Black women, who have not taken seriously the root meaning of the term womanist. According to Hill, womanists love other women regardless of their sexuality, or emotional flexibility. The lesbian voice is silenced by Christian womanist theologians.

Hill wonders if the silence of Christian womanist theologians is due to their location in the Christian church. "There is no widespread discussion of sexuality in African-American theology in general. Christian womanists, like their male counterparts, focus for the most part on the impact of racism on the Black community. The Christian womanist focus on gender is to a great degree a focus on the retrieval of Black women's stories, words and perspectives. There is no great emphasis on the impact of sexism on the black community. This may be the key to the lack of discourse on sexuality."[34] Many Black churches dismiss issues of sexuality as giving in to the lower nature of people and as representative of the influence of the outside world. Additionally, there are churches that maintain that sexuality, especially as it relates to gay and lesbian issues, is a White issue that has no place in the Black community particularly the Black church. Further, if there is a problem regarding sexuality, Christians should be careful not to air "their dirty laundry in public." Hill is insistent that Christian womanist theologians are missing an opportunity to represent issues of sexuality that are pressing in the Black community. "Sexuality is an issue for Christian womanist theologians. It is not any less or any more important than community or survival. It simply is a part of community and survival. Sexuality (and male dominance) must be discussed in the Black community. Only then will we be able to discuss subjects like rape, the AIDS epidemic, as well as sexual orientation in the Black community."[35]

At the Christian theological school where I teach there is a marked change in confronting issues of oppression of gay and lesbian others. The school is clear that all forms of oppression, which includes the marginalization of minorities, are unacceptable. What I find interesting is that there is no appeal to a Christian ethos as a framework for talk about sexuality. The framework is civil and human rights. All human beings by virtue of being human have rights in relation to the privileges and responsibilities that are inherent in being a university community. Perhaps one reason why a Christian school has not proffered a Christian frame of reference for how minorities are treated, and in this case, gay and lesbian others, is the uncertainty of where the church stands and how the church will react. Martin Luther King, Jr. observed some years ago that in relation to social issues the church is often more "like the tail lights rather than the head lights." The church is often reactive rather than proactive in relation to social issues.

Also, I find it interesting that at the university where I work, much leadership in our response to issues of sexuality comes from our students rather than our faculty. Faculty seem rather unsure how far to go, and they worry about what may or may not be acceptable to the church. At this university we have had a history in which the church has intervened at the highest level of university administration and stipulated what practices are to be allowed and under what circumstances on campus. There is, then, a sense in which the Christian identity as it relates to the university and college serves as a barrier for genuine airing of the issues of sexuality, especially as it relates to lesbians and gays. In this context, leadership often comes from the students who constitute themselves in student organizations and seek to place issues of their survival before the community. In the classes I teach the most fruitful discussion on issues of sexuality as it pertains to the oppression of lesbians and gays often occur because gay and lesbian students are willing to risk, as they self-identify, and press the class to clarify how we respond to them as persons. Usually, a good half of the class is uncertain how to respond and others are very tentative.

There is an urgent need for leadership in the classroom and church as we struggle with issues of emancipatory pedagogy, the practice of teaching and learning that is liberatory. The school and church are not yet clear on our stance regarding the ordination of gay and lesbian persons for the Christian ministry. Hill raises hard questions for the practice of liberation as she counsels her Christian womanist colleagues that womanist theology must include liberation for gays and lesbians within the Black community.

Hill reminds us that the central question that will move women forward in ways of mutuality is: "Who are we for ourselves and for each other?" According to Hill, as women take their experience seriously as a point of departure for action/reflection aimed at transforming community, they will nurture each other, challenge patriarchal structures, and love each other. Care for the community must include self-care. Black women must take time to love themselves. "Mutuality, self-determination and self-love can give Christian womanists the power and the resources to claim sexuality as an important issue for theology, spirituality and justice making in the Black community. This is especially important, for Christian womanists who, if they are going to be true to Walker's definition of womanism, must be willing to listen to the lesbian voice."[36]

Hill's call to Christian womanist theologians to listen to the voice of lesbians and gay persons in the community means among other things that the penchant for denial of gay and lesbian persons in the Black church/Black community must come to an end. Womanist theology must not imitate Black church practice in this regard and pretend that issues of Black sexuality are imported from the White feminist community. As lesbians and gay folk are embraced by the community they will cease to be invisible and will be given the power to name their own reality. One of the profound challenges for womanist theology is to begin to struggle with what it would mean to include the experience of lesbian others in such a way that their reality begins to shape the outcome of this theology.

What would it look like for womanist theology if the lesbian experience is at the center and not the periphery of womanist ways of knowing and being in the world? What would liberation look like in the Black community? In what ways would talk about love, faith, and justice be different? What would a conversation with the Black church look like? It would force the Black church to confront issues of denial and invisibility that are a symptom of oppression in the Black church. Hill names the risks and possibilities of an inclusive hermeneutic of the Black womanist experience:

> Listening to the lesbian voice would also compel the Black community to challenge the different sexual stereotypes and images that have been assigned to Black women. The lesbian has been regarded by many as either inadequate or dangerous. Inadequate because, according to the stereotype, she does not produce children (in reality lesbians, like all other women, may or may not have children; may or may not want children). Dangerous because she challenges compulsory heterosexuality and she may also challenge male supremacy depending on her politics. The lesbian is seen as "other." Her otherness has been such a powerful source of fear that she has had to be made invisible, her liberation and well-being made non-issues. But in looking directly into the eyes of the "other" and by listening to her voice, womanist may find the tools to re-examine and do away with not only lesbian stereotypes, but also other negative images of Black women (the "Mammy," the "whore" and the baby maker for example).[37]

Hill accuses Christian womanist theologians for contributing to the invisibility of lesbians by refusing to acknowledge them and include them within the framework of the Black womanist experience. She points out that when theologians seem to fear lesbians as lesbians, then they are often referred to as others. One way of overcoming this fear is the invitation to love lesbians, to look into their eyes and allow the stereotypes that shroud their being to be removed as lesbians are accorded their rightful place in the Black community/Black church. Womanist theologians are admonished to construct theology that speaks to the exclusion of lesbians from the Christian and wider communities.

By including lesbians at the center of the Black womanist experience, womanist theologians will begin to unravel the stereotypes of lesbians as inadequate and dangerous, which are pervasive in the Black church/Black community. This will begin an examination of ways of speaking about Black women in the wider community as "mammy," "whore," and baby maker. Black women will thereby begin to seize the opportunity to identify themselves as they name their own world. In a church and society in which others often represent Black women by speaking for them and act on their behalf, womanist theology calls attention to emancipatory speech and action in which women represent themselves. Women are able to look at reality, including God, from a womanist point of view. But womanist scholar Hill warns that even as women seek to represent themselves, they have to guard against marginalizing lesbian sisters. The experience of the struggle of women against injustice as this is enabled and enriched by the stories of women must include all sisters within the Black community. Womanist scholars are challenged to name God and emancipatory praxis out of their own social location in such a way that transformation and liberation are inclusive of the entire community.

3

Pedagogy and Ontological Sameness

We have noted the difficulty of Black and womanist theologies seeking to provide ways of knowing and being that foster empowerment for all members of the Black community. As the story of Black and womanist theologies unfold, we are told that Black theologians sought to fashion God-talk as a way of accessing the power of self-determination and liberation from the onslaught of White racism, and as a way to plan a new future for all members of the Black community. Most Black theologians spoke and acted out of the Christian tradition, and as a consequence sought to relate the message of Jesus to the search for freedom in the Black community. Some of the theologians who were preeminent in the articulation of this new Black theology of empowerment for the Black community were James Cone, J. Deotis Roberts, Major Jones, and Gayraud Wilmore. All of these theologians regarded the Black church as the locus and home of Black theology. We noted that one of the reasons given for the necessity of Black theology was that White religionists in their attempt to relate the message of Jesus to the existential situation in which they worked and lived did not include the Black religious experience of suffering and oppression as raw material for the construction of God-talk. Black theologians observed that it was difficult for them to do otherwise as they engaged in God-talk in a context of White supremacy, and in this context it was virtually impossible for them to value the suffering and struggle of oppressed Black people in their efforts to talk about God and reality.

According to Black theologians, White theologians rendered Black people invisible as they refused to allow their pain and pathos, their struggle for meaning in a White racist world to shape God-talk. This meant, among other things, that in the United States of America, the attempt of White religionists to engage in God-talk was not from the perspective of the tragic in society. Their theologies could not be a genuine representation of the cross of Christ as they failed to see the identification of the Christ of the gospels with the tragic and the grotesque represented in Black life. These theologians were unable to relate the gospel of Jesus to oppressed Black people who suffer most under existing capitalist, patriarchal, and White supremacist social relations. Their theologies did not engage the social inequalities rife in the society.

Ostensibly, it was this need to connect God-talk with the most vulnerable in the society that made Black theologians contend that if theology was to be in the business of liberating God's children, then its point of departure had to be the cross of Christ manifest in the struggles and sufferings of Black people in the United States of America. On the one hand, Black theology emerged as a critique of the failure of White theology to relate the gospel of Christ to those who were locked out of access to scarce resources and locked into a battle to defeat circles of death, and to sustain life.

It is worth noting that perhaps the first book in the contemporary expression of liberation theology, *Black Theology and Black Power,* was released in 1969, a year after the death of Martin Luther King, Jr., and four years after the death of Malcolm X. Issues of Black rage and feelings of powerlessness were an important part of the sociopolitical reality. Yet, what is interesting is that the emergent Black theology represented here, with its strident voice and claim that in "the twentieth century Christ meant Black power," did not shut the door of dialogue on White religionists and theologians. They were invited to dialogue, and in conversation they were held accountable for crafting and expounding God-talk within the context of racist assumptions in relation to Black people. What is the origin of this openness of Black theologians to White religionists who rendered them invisible? Is this embrace of the stranger an overflow of the inclusive love of the Black church? I would like to tease out in this chapter the implications for pedagogy.

Black theologians did not seek to practice an exclusionary pedagogy in relation to White religionists. However, our conversation with womanist theologians reveals that they did not have a similar experience in relation to Black theologians; their experience was one of exclusion. In embracing the White stranger, Black theologians excluded the Black woman as friend, mother, sister, and theologian. At one level, we inquire whether the sociological reality of sameness—Black women belonging to the same race, in many cases the same religion, same country, shared suffering and similarities in terms of history and culture—was partly to blame for the invisibility of Black women in Black theology. We inquire if it were the case that Black theologians did not make a connection between immanence and transcendence in their understanding of Black women. There is a sense in which the unknowability of the White stranger pressed Black theologians to see otherness (transcendence) in the stranger, while focusing on the shared similarities of Black women as friend, mother, sister made them concentrate not on the transcendence of the friend, but on issues of sameness, immanence, and knowability.

However, as we listened to womanist theologians in earlier chapters, there seems to have been a deeper and more pervasive problem: the attempt of Black theologians to speak for all Black people from the perspective of the so-called Black experience. This was an understandable flaw in the construction and articulation of Black theology. The intent of Black theologians was to be all-inclusive and so to construct God-talk from the Black experience of suffering and struggle for freedom and meaning in the United States of America was a very honest way to represent the entire Black community. It seemed very natural for Black male theologians to speak for the entire Black community as they were drawing from the Black religious experience. The implications for pedagogy are very clear. As teachers do we run the risk often of seeking to speak for the class from the perspective of a collective sharing and experience? In what sense, if any, are students allowed to represent their perspectives, to reflect and share from their experience often of powerlessness?

Womanist theologians helped us see that Black male theologians got it wrong on a number of scores. For one, the experience from which they were drawing was the Black male experience because they continued to talk about God and reality in male terms, which meant that their language was not liberating for women. Black women were neither consulted, nor were they given the opportunity to name their own reality, to speak from their own experience. The problem here was that Black male theologians spoke from an imagined shared reality with women in an attempt to construct an "imagined community."

Not only was the language male, and hence not representative of women, but the experiences of Black women were excluded. Black women could not see themselves in the attempt of Black theologians to speak on their behalf. Further, our attempt to talk about God and reality from the Black perspective and experience was as oppressive as White religionists who spoke and theologized from a religious universal.

Professor Jacquelyn Grant pointed out that the problem was that the Black religious experience functioned as a kind of universal in which identities were lost, and she wonders why Black women believe that the work of Black religious scholars would be any different for women when what Black theologians did was to take over a White frame of reference and seek to make it applicable to the Black religious experience. In many cases, the methodology employed by Black theologians was taken over from White religionists. Allow me to mention that this is one of the concerns that haunts me in my attempt to teach the social sciences. Often, I raise the question of to what extent students are able to see themselves represented in the literature. In a recent attempt at teaching systematic theology, I decided to place on the classroom video screen a picture of the author of each text being discussed. It was most revealing to note the groups that were not represented in the pictures, especially when students cheered as they saw pictures that represented their race. The problem here is that it is often difficult for students to connect the subject matter being discussed with life and issues in their communities when they are not represented.

Black Woman's Struggle for Survival as Source

Womanist theologians found the work of Black male theologians inadequate and unacceptable as a liberation tool for Black women. The liberation project as conceived and articulated by Black theologians could not, with specificity, spell liberation for Black women because it did not connect with life as women know it in their experience, and in their struggle to survive. Linda E. Thomas argues that what was needed was an anthropological point of departure that gave an account of the lives of every day Black women. Thomas felt she had to guard against representing an elite class, albeit a Black elite class, as it did not spend time with working-class Black women. The truth is the issue was deeper than this claim by Thomas. The point was that Black women did not see themselves in the portrayal of the Black experience by Black men. It became clear that Black theology was well intentioned in that it sought through its reflection on the Black religious experience to construct God-talk that was representative of the entire community but failed miserably. It was precisely at this point that womanist theologians broke the silence and began to talk about theologizing from the framework of Black women's struggle for survival. Womanist theologians informed us that only Black women are able to do this work as other well-intentioned groups such as

White women and Black men cannot represent them. Black women must represent themselves and speak for themselves.

The implications for pedagogy are transparent as we begin to ask: What does it mean to represent others in the context of teaching and learning? What does it mean for an author to speak for self, to represent self in the context of the class? We sense these difficulties when we are dealing with ancient texts such as the Bible, or when we are trying to interpret traditions of the church. As we engage a first-century text how may we be sure that the representation taking place is authentic? Do we need to have access to original languages? Again, Thomas warns against the emergence of an elitist theology, as those who are able to do research and get their work published are often the middle class and upper middle class. Even if womanist theology proposes to speak for women, how may they be assured that they are speaking for all Black women?

To illustrate this difficulty, I recall an incident some years ago when renowned author Toni Morrison gave a wonderful and illuminating lecture at the American Academy of Religion conference. At the end of the lecture she met with Black women scholars who were in attendance. Many persons noted the irony in that Toni Morrison and these Black women scholars, as they engaged in scholarly discourse were served by Black women who worked at the hotel as domestic staff. The question being raised is: How may we prevent Black and womanist theologies from becoming middle-class enterprises that exclude working-class brothers and sisters? In what sense, if any, are these theologies expressions of God-talk from the perspective of the middle class? It is in this context we have to listen to womanist scholar Renee Hill as she presses womanist theology to engage in intratalk among other Black women, and in this case lesbians, whom she claims are not being included in womanist theology. How is the lesbian voice represented, and in what sense will the lesbian presence shape the outcome of womanist theology? Hill admonishes womanist theology not to ape the Black church in this regard and render the lesbian community invisible but to provide an agenda of liberation for the community that restores the humanity of all women. Womanists are challenged to love all women regardless.

The Passion for Ontological Sameness

I would like to attempt two things. First, I would like to tease out the implication of sameness providing a cover for invisibility and multiforms of oppression. Second, I would like to discover in theology and in pedagogy the ways in which we may invest perspectives of sameness with a culture of transcendence. I will engage the thought of Kimberly Simmons in her article, "A Passion for Sameness" in *Black Feminist Anthropology*.[1] To further explicate the relationship between Black suffering and pedagogy, we will look at an important essay by J. Deotis Roberts "The Wholeness of Humanity" and "Womanist Theology: Black Women's Experience as Source for Doing Theology, With Special Reference to Christology" by Jacquelyn Grant. Both essays raise the question of the meaning of transcendence that is always lurking at the door in the study of Black and womanist theologies.

Simmons reminds us of the dilemma of Black women throughout the history of America's struggle for freedom: "From their early involvement in the abolitionist and suffrage movements to their activism during the Civil Rights Movement, Black women have been at the center of the struggle for liberation for all Black people. Despite Black women's presence and contribution to the larger women's movement and the Civil Rights Movement, however, they have been mostly invisible in feminist research designed to document and illuminate women's lives and histories, mainly because the focus of the research has been on the experiences of White women—women being co-terminus with White."[2] This conjoining of women with Whiteness is seen throughout the discipline of anthropology Simmons argues, and it raises the question of Black women's power to alter this relationship. In this context of the lack of power to alter their invisibility in so-called Western anthropology, Simmons posits an oppositional and transformative approach aimed at reclaiming the centrality of sameness against the backdrop of difference and to refocus the importance of race and racial constructions in talk about gender and class.

To posit sameness as a starting point for anthropology, and I may dare say theology, is not a breakthrough as "conceptualization of sameness, importantly, began with an assertion of the universality of women's experience as constituted by their biological status as female," does not get at the uniqueness of the suffering of particular groups.[3] According to Simmons, the inappropriateness of the sameness method was exposed by Third World women scholars and activists who saw clearly that the unifying analytical theme of biology was conceptually, and, therefore, politically problematic. An important variable was the power relations embedded in the relationship of White feminists doing research in the Third World and the subjects they were studying. The notion of universality inherent in the concept of women broke down as issues of race and class forced them to begin to talk about different feminisms. "The shift from the idea of singular feminism to the acknowledgement of different feminisms was and is crucial to this change. Further, as feminist anthropology continues to explore how unequal power relations are created in the dynamics of anthropological research, women anthropologists can no longer afford to ignore the differences of education, resources, and mobility between themselves and their women subjects."[4] The fact that women are of the same gender does not erase power relationships and privileges inherent in these relationships. Simmons laments that the turn to difference instead of the embrace of sameness has not resulted in Black women breaking the silence; therefore the way forward is the "decolonizing" of anthropology and the articulation of a Black feminist anthropology.

I mentioned Simmons' assessment of the state of Western anthropology and the turn to Black feminist anthropology because it calls attention to the Black condition whether one looks through the prism of anthropology or from a theological perspective, and it begins to show up the inherent difficulties in an approach to the Black community, in terms of the conceptual construct of sameness or the notion of universality inherent in that claim. But this does not yet acknowledge issues of power relations extant even in the language we employ, in levels of education and often in socioeconomic terms. Black anthropologists complained that they and their community were invisible in the work done by White anthropologists. To belong to the same gender, they discovered, does not insulate one from invisibility. Even the turn to difference did not mean that they were included as equals because it did not address power relations between Black and White women. Simmons suggests the way forward:

> It is Black feminism's conscious and purposeful linking of theory and practice that enables us as scholars to place U.S. African American women and African and African Diaspora women at the center of conceptual framework that holds as central their lived experiences, histories, and the alliances they create. As a result, Black feminism stands at the crossroads of engaged scholarship, responsibility, and activism.[5]

It seems to me that another way to conceptualize the problem pointed to in Simmons' emphasis on sameness as a hermeneutical key is to note on the one hand, the limits of sameness as a heuristic tool, and on the other hand, the possibilities of sameness as a conceptual key.

Simmons speaks of the tension between sameness and difference, but it becomes more complicated for her as she talks about her research subjects in the Dominican Republic, who wanted her to be one of them, and then at the same time differentiating themselves from her. They acknowledged that she was one of them in physical looks, perhaps in the music she liked, yet they noted she was different in language. It was the stubborn refusal to limit sameness to the universal quality inherent in it, and to recognize that although she was of the same color, and perhaps religion, there was a quality of otherness to her that could not be ignored or coopted. I also find it interesting that Simmons wants to appeal to the universal quality inherent in the notion of sameness as she wants to articulate an ontology of sameness that includes Africans, African Americans, and the African Diaspora. But this ontology of sameness must delineate issues of race, gender, class, and nation. The notion of place was of first importance as people in the Dominican Republic wanted to know whether Simmons belonged here[Dominican Republic] or there[United States].

> My incorporation into Dominican society was neither seamless nor complete, of course, but these encounters highlight the complexity of Dominican's notions of themselves. Because I spoke Spanish with an English-language accent, for example, people questioned me about whether I was *de aqui o de alla* from here or from there (meaning the United States). The construction of *here* and *there* is the same way Dominicans conceptualize and acknowledge the presence of the Dominican Diaspora and classify relationships between Dominicans on the island and Dominicans in the United States. This construction may also be viewed as a narrative of authenticity, for within it is contained a clear delineation of who is Dominican and who is a "Dominican Dominican."[6]

I am grateful to anthropologist Simmons for including not only race, gender, and class in the analysis of ontological sameness, but also nation because the vantage point from which one sees the world determines one's angle of vision. An identity shaped by race, gender, class, and nation provides a focal point for talk about integrity and centeredness in the Black community. For Dominicans, according to Simmons, a sense of place whether one is from here or there determines how one sees the world. As place is included, one now sees the world not only through a different pair of lenses, but from a different place. Therefore, the Dominicans ask are you *de aqui o de alla*? Are you from here or from there? The answer determines how your identity is interpreted.

According to Simmons, the problem with being from there (the United States), is that Dominicans see you as having a watered-down identity. The identity is watered down because it is not interpreted in relation to them. One's primary identity must be seen in relation to themselves. The converse was true for Simmons because she was from the United States and wants to understand Dominicans in relation to the African Diaspora from where she self-identified. Not so with Dominicans, they wanted to understand her in relationship to themselves.

> ...my early attempts to self-define as African American or Black were often met with looks of disapproval and expressions of disbelief. I was told that I needed to be proud of my Dominican heritage, of who I was and where I came from, even if I was born *alla*. This contestation over my identity and origins usually persuaded me to assume an *India Clara* (and sometimes *mulatta*) identity in the Dominican Republic, especially because this is how others define me in relation to themselves.[7]

The bottom line has to do with the ingredients that go into the way we self-define. To what extent do we see ourselves the way others see us?

As one who hails from the island of Jamaica in the Caribbean, I can relate to the double identities of being from here (United States and African Diaspora) and there (Jamaica). But the determining factor for Jamaicans at home as to how they understand my identity has to do with my embrace of the culture, especially as this is translated in my ability to communicate the language. Although I was born in Jamaica and attended high school, theological seminary, and pastored churches there, was married and raised a family on the island, there is something of a rupture in the ontology of sameness for Jamaicans at home as they talk about my identity because I live there and not here, and my facility with the native dialect points to the distance between here and there. The rupture has to do with the place from which I write and work and points to the limits of sameness. There is a sense in which the rupture created a distance between sameness and otherness, between immanence and transcendence. There is a sense that unless you belong here and not there, as people define you in relation to themselves, then you have lost transcendence, you have lost identity.

As we consider this frame of reference and its applicability to Black and womanist theologies, I would like to turn now to the two essays mentioned earlier, one by Black theologian J. Deotis Roberts and the other by womanist theologian Jacqueline Grant in search for a sense of how they understand their discipline relative to ontological sameness: whether in terms of here or there, whether they focus on the African American community in the United States, or whether they reference the African Diaspora or the Christian church as the space that shapes identity. We will investigate the place from which they talk about community and in what way this point of departure affects their angle of vision. How do they reference issues of shared similarity and what are the limits and possibilities for learning and teaching?

Linking the Theological and the Sociological

As a way of linking the theological with the sociological, I would like us to travel with J. Deotis Roberts as he gives us a sense of what it means to talk about humanity from a Black theological perspective during the formative years of Black theology. Roberts speaks of "The Wholeness of Man [Humanity]" in Chapter 3 of his important text, *A Black Political Theology.*[8] He begins his essay on the wholeness of humanity that finds its locus in what he calls the Biblical understanding of humanity. He casts his net very wide as he begins with the human situation of faith and its role in shaping Black identity. His ontology of sameness focuses on a shared quality of all of God's children: whether from here or from there, who are imbued with this divine quality called the image of God. Remembering the language of Victor Anderson in his book *Beyond Ontological Blackness,*[9] we could speak of the starting point of Roberts' approach as beyond ontological sameness as he wants to begin with a common universal condition of wholeness grounded in the image of God. Although he begins beyond ontological sameness he hurries to the desecration and despoiling of the human condition as is manifest in the tragic expressed in slavery in the United States, and reminds us of the important work by H. Shelton Smith, *In His Image, But....* The Biblical image of God in all persons takes Black theology beyond a sense of place and forces Black theology beyond ontological sameness as Roberts concretely relates the despoiling of this image in the American South in the disturbing phrase, "In His image, but." Roberts begins by pointing to the limits of ontological sameness. Ontological sameness points beyond here and there, but is limited to space and place as it provides anthropological grounding for talk about the human condition. Roberts wants to push beyond here and there as bases for location of identity and relate human beings to the divine as locus and focus of identity.

The relating of human identity to the divine image allows for the transcendence of geography whether construed as here or there, but the bifurcation between here and there points to the rupture in wholeness or in ontological sameness. He lifts up for us the threat and the promise of ontological sameness as articulated by Simmons. The threat has to do with the split between here and there; the promise has to do with the necessity of space and place in talking about the vocation to be human. However, it is important to note that if there is a problem in seeking to fashion an understanding of wholeness on the basis of sociological concreteness, Roberts also sees a problem in divorcing the theological from the sociological. The dilemma is that slavery and racism in the American South distorted the image of God and the task of Black theology is to illustrate a way back to wholeness, a way that restores the image of God in Black humanity.

Roberts suggests a new way of talking about humanity. In the United States of America the way the dominant culture and religion talk about Black humanity is to imply: made in the image of God, but.... Roberts postulates a tension between here and there. Here in the United States of America, Black humanity is demeaned and dehumanized, but there in the land from which African Americans hail, the theological and the sociological are conjoined. Here human beings are spoken of in terms of the tension between body and soul, the body belongs to the master while the soul belongs to God. For Roberts, in Africa there is a unity of body and soul, the individual and the collective, the spiritual and the physical, divinity and humanity. "There is a unity of all life. Man is vitally related to nature, God, ancestors, and the like. He enters into the whole of being, without dividing up into parts. The African is fully conscious of the wholeness and cohesiveness of the whole of creation, within which interaction is the only way to exist."[10]

The limits of the ontology of sameness point to the alienation and estranged existence that is the common lot of African Americans in the United States of America, due to racism and slavery, according to Roberts. The possibilities of restoration are made plain in the African worldview in which the rupture between the theological and the sociological are conjoined. Because the liberation project, as Roberts sees it, is to relate the quest for liberation from this negative sense of self and community expressed in the notion, "In His image, but...," liberation must be conjoined with a vision of wholeness and the relating of the theological and the social, restoring the rupture is to make peace with here and there. This attempt to articulate a theology of wholeness is especially poignant for persons who experience the university or college context as alien. And part of the reason for this alienation is what we are calling the rupture of ontological sameness, the separation in terms of the way we have defined ourselves and the attempt of our new, alien culture/context to define us in relation to itself and to limit the interpretation of self to either a theological or sociological interpretation. In this context Roberts takes us back to the depth of Black culture, to talk about our ancestors and a way of being and knowing that is constitutive to our identity as whole persons. The first strategy that Roberts employs in the face of the rupture of how we know ourselves and how others seek to define us is to appeal to roots. Let us identify ourselves in terms of our roots. Do we know ourselves as our parents know us?

In my Jamaican culture there is a saying that a tree cannot be so important that it forgets its roots or regard its roots as unimportant. For a tree to be whole and strong it has to care for roots. Roberts explains:

> The term *ujamaa* is used in East Africa to refer to "familyhood." Man cannot be whole without the experience of community as fulfillment. God has created us for sociability and this is the very essence of man as man. Social consciousness is built into the very nature of Christian anthropology. Black theology is concerned for the liberation of the oppressed in the social setting where men must find authentic existence.[11]

Roberts is very helpful in reminding us that human beings and in this case Black humanity, must experience authentic liberation in the social setting in which one seeks to make meaning. This means that it is helpful to look to Africa for roots and for images of wholeness, but existence is lived in the crucible of Black life under the banner of racism. The struggle has to be waged in the place in which one stands, works, and plays. In my research on Jamaican spirituality, we encountered a similar problem among the Rastafari who also witnessed to the rupture between here and there, between life in Jamaica and their hope for African redemption. In their search for wholeness they looked to African roots to help them resolve their difficulty with "Babylonian captivity." The Rastas regarded Jamaica and its commitment to a colonial way of life as Babylonian and claimed that wholeness, liberation, and the experience of an individuated self could not be found in the context of Jamaica because Jamaican institutions and government had sold out to the brokers of power who were against poor people. To use the language of anthropologist Simmons, they witnessed to the rupture between here and there, they identified self in relation, not to colonial powers or authorities, but to the emperor of Ethiopia, Haile Selassie I, in whom they claimed Christ had returned and God had revealed Godself for Black humanity. For the Rastas, authentic Black humanity was in terms of a relatedness to the Black man in Ethiopia, Haile Selassie I, who had become God for them.

It continues to be difficult for a people whose social setting is Jamaica to translate their dream of wholeness in relation to Africa and her traditions when the possibility of changing social location is not practical, and even if they could change social location there would still be the tension between the here they embody and their trying to make Ethiopia home. They have begun to plan a new future as they are now beginning to say that Africa is in Jamaica, that as they incorporate African traditions in their social situation they begin to bridge the distance between here and there, the theological and the sociological, and create space for the emergence of ontological sameness. The claiming that Africa is in Jamaica, where here and there are conjoined in the Jamaican situation, provides the basis for a social consciousness that helps them question reality in that context. The turn to Africa was a turn to wholeness as it enabled them to conjoin traditions of spirituality with social reality as they struggle for meaning in their existential context.

The Turn to the Christian Story

If one way of healing the rupture between here and there, between living with a sense of limits on the one hand and possibilities on the other is to identify self, personal and collective self, in relationship to African roots, to see ourselves the way our ancestors understand us, it becomes clear that for Roberts a more poignant strategy to effect healing in our understanding of ontological sameness is to identify self, personal and collective, in relation to the Christian story. Black theology as it fashions a new humanity so to speak must use as source and resource African history and culture. It is in this context that Black theology understands as one of its primary roles the relating of the liberation motif to the search for wholeness and wholesomeness, culturally and historically mediated. The search to conjoin here and there, existence in the new world and being torn away from African roots, is emblematic of life in the New World. The new status of

Africans in the New World as slaves points to a new existence marked by separation between here and there. No wonder enslaved people would cry, "Way down yonder by myself I couldn't hear nobody pray." The absence of family in Africa, the longing for the forests, all point to an experience of hell in the new social context. Hell was separation between here and there, it signaled the loss of ontological oneness. One strategy to conjoin here and there was to remember Africa in whose traditions the theological and the sociological inhere. Some enslaved persons practiced suicide, believing that in death they returned to Africa to be reunited with family and the forests. I recall so very vividly when I first migrated to the United States to study how I longed for the forests and the mountains in Jamaica. For many years every night when I retired to sleep I would dream of the mountains and the forests, and so I began to look forward to my dreams as a way to return home to be with the forests and the ancestors. Perhaps this explains why enslaved persons would sing: "Steal away, steal away, I haven't got long to stay here." When life in the here is hell, one longs for there.

The critical question on the mind of J. Deotis Roberts as he turns to Christianity as a tool for liberation is whether Christianity as presented by the oppressor class could be used as a tool for survival. Does this religion as presented by the White missionary and preacher have within it the substance to provide healing for Africans in the New World who are ripped from home and taken through the middle passage to these new shores? Roberts explains a dilemma that Africans in the New World had with the Christianity presented by the White preacher:

> Even during slavery, when blacks were still in chains, Paul's exhortation: "Slave, obey your masters" (Col.3:22) became a favorite text for slavery preachers and theologians. Paul could sincerely request that Philemon receive his slave Onesimus ("useful," "beneficial") as a slave in the flesh, but as a brother in the Lord (Philemon 16). The position of Paul on master-slave relations became the standard proclaimed by slavery Christianity in reference to blacks. Paul has not been fully appreciated by several black religious thinkers. Howard Thurman and Albert Cleage agree on this point.[12]

Howard Thurman corroborates Roberts' assessment of his questions concerning Paul's view of Christianity, and the many questions raised by Black people concerning its appropriateness for Black liberation. In his important text, *Jesus and the Disinherited*, Thurman points out that he finds very little help in navigating everyday existence in the teachings of the church concerning Jesus Christ. In his generation there is a sense that the church failed Africans in the New World in their quest for meaningful existence as the teachings of Jesus were tailored for the strong and powerful in the society, and not for the weak and oppressed. Thurman tells of growing up with his grandmother who was born into slavery and recounts how she would always ask him to read from the Bible.

> During much of my boyhood I was cared for by my grandmother, who was born a slave and lived until the Civil War on a plantation near Madison, Florida. My regular chore was to do all of the reading for my grandmother—she could neither read nor write. Two or three times a week I read the Bible aloud to her. I was deeply impressed by the fact that she was most particular about the choice of Scripture. For instance, I might read many of the more devotional Psalms, some of Isaiah, the Gospels again and again. But the Pauline epistles, never—except, at long intervals, the thirteenth chapter of First Corinthians...When I was older and was half through college, I chanced to be spending a few days at home near the end of summer vacation. With a feeling of great temerity I asked her one day why it was that she would not let me read any of the Pauline letters. What she told me I shall never forget. "During the days of slavery," she said, "the master's minister would occasionally hold services for slaves. Old man McGhee was so mean that he would not let a Negro minister preach to the slaves. Always the white minister used as his text something from Paul. At least three or four times a year he used as a text: 'Slaves, be obedient to them that are your masters....', as unto Christ. Then he would go on to show how it was God's will that we were slaves and how, if we were good and happy slaves, God would bless us. I promised my Maker that if I ever learned to read and if freedom ever came, I would not read that part of the Bible."[13]

Thurman poses for us the critical question that Roberts seeks to answer: how can the religion of Jesus that was used as weapon to validate "In His image, but ..." also function as a tool for healing and restoration?

Roberts points out that even in the context of the church, White Christians had to struggle with whether salvation and freedom were related. If enslaved persons became saved did that mean they were free? "This was settled in a negative statement by a Virginia court: conversion and emancipation do not take place at the same time."[14]

According to Roberts the church used Paul to provide a theological base that insisted that slaves could be free in the Lord and remain shackled in the chains of physical bondage. This position is still maintained by a number of churches that maintain an inherent inferiority of Black people. Roberts suggests that Black people need to have a hermeneutic of suspicion when dealing with the White church's interpretation of scripture. It is in this context that Black theology seeks to develop a theology of Black consciousness: an awareness of the insidiousness of racism and the ways in which it masks itself as being for the salvation of Black souls. Not only should Africans in the Diaspora be on the look out for the deception and masking of racism, but also Africans on the continent. "Many Africans need to decolonize their minds. They are too trusting of their former exploiters. In many cases they have accepted without question the values of the colonizers." In an ingenious way, Roberts calls attention to the problem of racism in both social situations. Whether here or there, the problem of racism is one for which Africans or Blacks in the African Diaspora have to be alert. The suggestion that Africans also need what Roberts calls a "gospel of deliverance" is surprising to many Blacks in the Diaspora as we are accustomed to look to Africa as that mythic homeland from which we may tap into traditions that are pure. This means that healing of the rupture in ontological sameness is not a one-way street. It means that Africa also needs the Diaspora in as much as the Diaspora needs Africa, and along those lines Roberts suggests that a Black theology is necessary as a way of raising the consciousness of oppression in Africa. "What I hope to see is a recognition of this 'common cause' in the transatlantic discussion between Blacks and African theologians."[15]

What is proffered is not an either or reaching out to the other, but mutual sharing of resources as a way of rooting out a common enemy. The goal is an ontology of sameness, a recognition of shared similarities, the making of common ground. But the existential situation presses us beyond our own resources. The bottom line is that Africans at home or in the African Diaspora need to identify themselves not only in relation to each other, but to affirm a sense of shared similarities and a need for mutuality. Because there is a sense in which the resources in each existential situation are inadequate to fashion a community in which wholeness and wholesomeness are reality, the hope for the combining of here and there, the hope for transatlantic solidarity is the way forward. The reality that hangs like a nightmare over many Black people is that Black life in a culture of White supremacy presses for a new future.

White mobs hanged, shot, burned, gouged, flogged, drowned, impaled, dismembered, and blowtorched to death almost 550 blacks, including aged cripples, young boys, and pregnant mothers, in lynchings from 1919 to 1939. Devout Protestants were among the participants at these "modern Golgothas." These would-be servants of the Lord encouraged or silently acquiesced in lynchings. These evangelical Protestants saw no relationship between these acts of human torture and their deep piety. They were against smoking, drinking, and illicit sex. They closed down pool rooms, but they were silent on lynchings.[16]

The critical question for Black theology as it engages pedagogy and as it seeks to heal the rupture between here and there and restore wholeness and wholesomeness to ontological sameness is to claim the mutuality between Africans in the Diaspora and African traditions and history. For Roberts, the theology of solidarity means to interpret Black existence in the light of God "the giver and redeemer of life." It is clear that Roberts sees the God factor as the main key in which the unity and wholeness of ontological sameness must be set. "The black man's dignity is not dependent on the whims and fancies of those who are his oppressors. Black men's awareness of their self-worth is not dependent on the findings of men such as Arthur Jensen, who would base the black man's low status in society upon inheritance through genes. Neither will we base our self-understanding upon a faulty theology that traces this inferiority to either God's ordained or permissive will. We know we are 'somebody.' God created us as 'somebody.' He sustains and redeems us as beings of supreme worth. We are not limited to man's estimate of man."[17]

It is clear that as important as it is for Blacks in the Diaspora to place their anthropologies and theologies in conversation with African history and traditions and vice versa, it is not a theology of solidarity or understandings of shared suffering and similarities that is the key to the reversal of the rupture in notions of ontological sameness, but God's estimate of Black humanity as children of God that has been tested in the fires of Black faith and hope in the dignity and sanctity of Black struggle and suffering. "It is against this background that through faith and the understanding of selfhood we have affirmed the dignity and infinite value of black life under God. We need an understanding of human nature that can bring to black people, under the conditions of their existence, sanity and wholeness."[18]

The psychic wounds and existential anguish of Black life are too overwhelming for Black humanity to create an anthropology of wholeness and Black dignity. This existential absurdity that confronts us in Black life has to be interpreted in the light of the grace of God as God enters creatively and redemptively into the Black condition.

Roberts gives us a feel for the existential absurdity that confronts Black humanity:

> The man with a black face who packs his lunch daily and waits on the edge of the city to bargain for a day's work with a white boss understands of what I speak. The black mother who leaves her little ones before daybreak to catch a bus to the suburbs to care for the children and the homes of the rich and the powerful in order to buy bread and pay rent, but who is too tired at eventide to feed and love her own children, can understand our meaning. In interpreting man in Christian theological perspective, the black theologian has to bring a meaning of self-respect to people who can no longer accept themselves.[19]

There is something of a dialectical tension for Roberts as he helps us construct language to bridge the distance between here and there, between an ability to talk about self in relation to the community we find in our own social setting or the larger Black community in the African and African Diaspora. He points to the limits of ontological sameness—that is whether we interpret self from the context of our own social setting or the African Diaspora, we encounter a negative estimate of self. We bump ourselves against racism on the one hand, or on the other hand we experience a negative sense of self, we discover that we are unacceptable to ourselves and to others who interpret us in the light of themselves.

It seems to me that Roberts allows for the possibility that on good days we reach for the best in our traditions and in our communities, whether here or there, and this is indispensable as we seek to see self in the light of roots, whether in our contextual situation or in the light of Africa and the African Diaspora. My sense is that this positive use of the traditions and sense of roots is the crucible for construction of a theological anthropology that spells ontological sameness. This is where immanence (here) and transcendence (there) meet. But for Roberts the negative and positive use of ontological sameness is not enough to bear the weight of the existential absurdity that plagues Black existence. This must be coupled with the witness of the ancestors and the Black community to the presence of the divine in acts of liberation. The good news is that questions about the humanity of the Black community lead us to the witness of the Black community concerning "the humanity of God." Black suffering forces the question: Does God care? The answer of the mothers and fathers of our faith and of the ecclesial community is that God cares. This faith in a God who cares coupled with a robust confidence in the traditions and faith of the ancestors provides healing of the rupture between immanence and transcendence, and bridges the distance between here and there in ontological sameness.

Christ Becoming Black Woman

The mood changes when we turn to Jacqueline Grant's article, "Womanist Theology: Black Women's Experience as a Source for Doing Theology, With Special Reference to Christology."[20] Grant speaks of the split in ontological consciousness occasioned by the triple evils of racism, sexism, and classism. To ignore any one of these evils is to forfeit the opportunity to work for holistic and integrated reality of Black womanhood. Although Grant insists on the priority of Black women's experience in crafting this theology of wholeness, what I find different here is her insistence that class analysis is the crucible on which liberation of the oppressed turns, those at the bottom of society, the Black and White poor must be included. What is important for our purposes is the turn to class as a critical category in the construction of a community in which ontological sameness inheres. This community that Grant advocates and sees womanist ways of knowing and being in the world as engendering, transcends race and gender because it includes poor people in the community, those at the bottom of the society, those who are most vulnerable, poor Black men, and poor White women. Grant explains:

> This means that Black women, because of oppression determined by race and their subjugation as women, make up a disproportionately high percentage of the poor and working classes. However, the fact that Black women are a subjugated group even within the Black community and the White women's community does not mean that they are alone in their oppression within those communities. In the women's community, poor White women are discriminated against, and in the Black community, poor Black men are marginalized. This suggests that classism as well as racism and sexism, has a life of its own. Consequently, simply addressing racism and sexism is inadequate to bring about total liberation…Classism impacts Black women in a peculiar way which results in the fact that they are most often at the bottom of the social and economic ladder.[21]

Grant reminds us that Black and Third World theologies exposed the hidden agenda of many versions of so-called classical theologies that claimed that they spoke for a universal understanding of humankind.

The invisible crucible that informed their God-talk was the dominant culture, as God-talk often told us more about the theologians and their culture than it told us about God or humanity. We learned from them a long time ago that theology is not unrelated to the sociopolitical situation of theologians even when they deny that this is the case.

Historically, much of so-called classical theology has been in the service of the status quo. This was the problem with God-talk that advocated the affirmation of a universal God. The problem with a universal God is that this God threatened and negated indigenous expressions of the divine and the negation of indigenous cultures. "Nowhere was this more clear than in the area of Christian foreign missions where conversion to Christianity implicitly meant the deculturalization and acceptance of the Western value system on the part of Asians, Africans, and Latin Americans. Upon conversion, one had to withdraw from indigenous ways of imagining the divine reality, and embrace foreign, western ways which often served to under-gird oppressive religious, social and political structures."[22] The universal portrayal of God was a local view of God disguised as universal, one that reflected the dominant culture. This God became an outsider and was unable to empower indigenous people in their fight for liberation. This view of God furthers and deepens the alienated view of personhood in the community. The view of God expressed by a theology that does not emerge from the people's history and culture diminishes and dehumanizes the community's view of self, personally and collectively, mediated through their symbols.

Another way in which the self is alienated and separated from the indigenous culture and history is in the attempt of Western theologians and missionaries to talk about love that is unrelated to issues of justice and power in the community. This attempt to divorce love from issues of justice and power often serves the interest of the guardians of the status quo and eviscerates notions of Black personhood that are essential for a holistic view of the Black community.

Grant points out that feminists, in similar fashion as Black theologians, offer an important critique of love as selflessness that is counterproductive for women as they seek to provide healing and wholeness in women's communities. Many Western theologians often portray sin as self-assertiveness and love as selflessness; this interpretation represents a masculine experience and does not address the experience of women. In order for ontological sameness and full personhood to be realized in the community, women's experience must be central. This view of sin as self- assertiveness and love as selflessness has the net result of keeping women in their place—that is in the home and out of leadership positions in society and church. For women to take these male theologians seriously it would mean for them to deny themselves. "Must women deny themselves in order to be saved?" Is this the price of ontological sameness? On the contrary, Black and feminist theologians get to the heart of the matter in pointing out that the universal that White theologians articulate is nothing more than the White religious and male experience parading as universal. This view of the universal is unable to unite that which is separated in the experience of ontological sameness because it represents a limited worldview.

What is interesting for our purposes as we seek to navigate our way into talk about wholesomeness and the relationship of personhood to matters of equity and reconciliation implicit in ontological sameness is that Grant observes that classical theologians may be on the right track in their insistence that universalism is a critical norm in talk about personhood in community. Along these lines womanist theology joins Black and feminist theology in their critique of so-called classical theology and at the same time provides an internal critique of these theologies in their search for insights from a womanist perspective.

Womanist theology joins feminist theology in the quest for a holistic theology that is not dependent on male ways of viewing the world and God. Male dominated theologies tend to be myopic as they do not value those who are excluded from the patriarchal way of viewing reality. A theology based on the male experience cannot provide healing for a fractured world and community because it represents a limited perspective. Further, the division in reality in which men are dominant and women are submissive must be eradicated, as a uniting of these perspectives is sought, if healing is to be effected. The division in reality is based in part on the dualistic view of reality in which men are regarded as strong, intelligent, rational, and aggressive and women are considered weak, fragile, and passive. Womanist theology joins feminist approaches to theology in conceptualizing and articulating new images of what it means to be woman. Racist and patriarchal ways of construing womanhood must be eliminated as new ways of understanding womanhood comes to the fore. Womanist theology is uniquely poised to lead the way in this new articulation and conceptualization of transformed personhood in which here and there, immanence and transcendence are conjoined.

The new perspective that womanist theology brings to the fore in the articulation of transformed humanity may be conceptualized from a number of perspectives. On the one hand, Grant and bell hooks[23] remind us that both the male and White female ways of construing the world and reality have been exclusionary of Black women. Male ways of being and knowing have been exclusionary of Black women, both from a racist and sexist perspective, and often as class issues impinge on Black women's existence, it is filtered through racist and sexist world-views. "Of course once class was placed on the agenda, women had to face the intersection of class and race. And when they did it was evident that black women were at the bottom of this society's economic totem pole."[24] Seeing race and gender issues filtered through class matters points up and points out that a disproportionately large number of Black women are excluded from the mainstream of society, and thereby make up the poor and working class. But it must be kept in mind that although Black women are at the bottom of the economic totem pole, they are joined by poor White women and poor Black men. It is "class matters" that points to the interlocking nature of race and gender oppression as it is expressed in the exclusion of poor people.

It is precisely in this context of the interlocking nature of race, sex, and class oppression that Grant and hooks remind us that class includes behavior, the assumptions that inform behavior, the pedagogy that informs behavior, the way one views the future and the estimate of self. Victims of class oppression usually have a very low view of self, which fosters feelings of passivity and restricted behavior—being forced to stay in one's place. The Black woman is the poster child so to speak of oppression that includes, race, sex, and class. "They share suffering with Black men; with white women and other Third world women, they are victims of sexism; and with poor Blacks and Whites, and other Third World peoples, especially women, they are disproportionately poor. To speak of Black women's tri-dimensional reality, therefore, is not to speak of Black women exclusively, for there is an implied universality which connects them with others."[25] There is an implied universality in Black women's suffering as it embraces the African Diaspora, here and there, Black and White, male and female. The point of departure for construal of the universality of suffering is the "least of these" as seen through the lens of class differentiation. It is those at the bottom of the social and economic totem pole that constitute a way of talking about oppression mediated by race, sex, and class that offer a way of talking about the oppression that fractures ontological sameness. Issues of equality, dignity, and justice and empowerment that have been placed on the margins as they relate to oppressed people are brought to the center in the quest for a new way of acting and being in community.

The way to spell wholeness and to mediate the values of dignity and sanctity for a new imaging of community is to discover Jesus Christ as poor, woman, and stranger. Jesus is able to bring together these disparate elements in community through solidarity with the "least of these." The definitive word about Black women is not that they are defined by issues of race, gender, and class, but that these issues represent the context of their struggle for liberation. It is in this context of oppression that Christ identifies with women, affirms their humanity, and engenders the hope for a liberated existence. As Christ is being formed in the community of women, Christ takes on the form of women. Grant reverses the old way of posing the Christological question in relation to women: What does it means for Christ to become like women? Rather than asking: What does it mean for women to become like Christ? She posits this as an appropriate question akin to first-century Palestine, when it was appropriate and expedient for Jesus the Christ to become a Jew—meaning to be iden- tified with the "least of these." In twentieth-century America, Black theologians depicted Jesus the Christ as Black male, and again Grant observes that this was appropriate, as the Black male was the symbol of marginalization and rejection. With the new reality of Black women being at the bottom of the social and economic totem pole and often being excluded by Black males and White women alike, Christ has to become Black woman and reveal Godself as mother, friend, wife, nur- turer, and suffering servant, despised and rejected by men. The Black woman in this society knows sorrow and grief and has borne society's transgressions and inequities. The Black woman is the means through whom God may make us whole.

At stake is the issue of ontological sameness—the common human- ity that informs and undergirds our search for wholeness and healing in our state of existential estrangement. At stake is a Christ who is fully human, who heals the brokenness and fragmented elements in our human family, and offers hope and liberation to all.

4

The Black Church and Pedagogy

When Black and womanist theologians call for the creation of communities in which people are free to witness the liberative power of the gospel of Christ in which there are not rigid distinctions between theory and practice, transcendence and immanence, the sacred and the secular, the call resonates with many Black Christians who know what these theologians mean. Indeed, it would be difficult to find a better example of the combination of profound trust in the breaking-in of new promises concerning what we may become as a people with concrete application to life in the social and political realm, than in the life of many Black churches in America. Perhaps this combination of future hope and concrete application to social and political realities has something to do with their roots in African thinking, which includes an unwillingness to adopt rigid time distinctions between past, present, and future that are found in conventional Western thinking.[1] The past and the future are drawn into the present in a way that makes it impossible to keep the dream of freedom from having a practical impact on the present. When Black people sang, "Swing Low, Sweet Chariot," they were expressing a profound religious experience; they were referring to an escape northward to freedom. "When the black slaves sang, 'I looked over Jordan and what did I see, Coming for to carry me home,' they were looking over the Ohio River."[2]

This unwillingness to put asunder what God has joined together—hope for a new future and the willingness to work to make it happen in the community—which characterizes the Black spiritual ethos—is what has uniquely equipped the Black church in its long march toward freedom and equality of Black people in this country. The only institution that could give birth to and sustain the Civil Rights Movement was the Black church. Before Black people went out on the streets to be beaten by cops and torn by dogs, they entered the door of the Black church to pray. It was not an accident that during the Civil Rights Movement in Mississippi thirteen Black churches were burned. The Black church had become not only the symbol of hope, but the agent of liberation for Black people. It was the awareness of the presence of the despised and rejected One in its midst that allowed the Black church to become the inspirational source, the organizational drive, and the sustaining power for a movement that might have often faltered and failed without the conviction that God was committed to the struggle to fashion a liberative community, and to enable the people to experience liberation in history. The solidarity of Christ with the community provided the shape of human hope for new ways of being and acting in community. Black people refused to give up on hope in spite of the oppressive context in which they had to eke out an existence. When Paul in Colossians 1:27 says that Christ is our hope, he makes a connection between hope and liberation for oppressed people. When oppressed people make the connection between hope and liberation, they struggle to free themselves from bondage because "the Lord their God is in the midst of them" (Deut. 7:21). The genius of Black people is that even in the shackles of oppression and slavery, they imagined a new community in which dignity and freedom were the fruits of struggle because "the Lord was in the midst of them." Then, hope must become historical liberation, and this is certainly why in the New Testament, hope is grounded in the incarnation of God, and why, as we seek to understand the hope for fruitful and meaningful community in the Black church, we turn to a review of the concrete history that shaped the Black experience.

Black History as Source for Liberation

Black people understood that although God was not limited to history, God was present in history as friend, mother, and hope for a new future. The God who became their liberator was one who suffered with them at the hands of an unjust oppressor. Enslaved persons were able to carve out an identity based on their relationship with God who joined them in their struggle and bestowed on them dignity and self-respect. The Black community was clear that God shared in their suffering. In a sense, this made their suffering bearable because the divine participated at the deepest level of their suffering. Black people's identification and participation in suffering was reciprocal. Because Christ identified with them they, in turn, identified with the cross of

Christ. At one level this begins to explain how they made it through the crucifixion of lynchings and rapes of dignity and self-respect. The prayer of an enslaved woman illustrates the confidence of oppressed Black people that Jesus cares for them:

> Dear Massa Jesus, we all uns beg Ooner [you] come make us a call dis yere day. We is nutting but poor Etiopian women and people ain't tink much 'bout we. We ain't trust any of dem great high people for come to we church, but do' you is de one great Massa, great too much dan Massa Linkum, you ain't shame to care for we African people.
>
> Come to we, dear Massa Jesus. De sun, he too hot too much, de road am dat long and boggy [sandy] and we ain't got no buggy for send and fetch Ooner [you]. But Massa, you member how you walked that hard walk up Calvary and ain't weary but tink about we all de way. We know you ain's weary for to come to we.[3]

According to this woman, Jesus identifies with poor Black people. He thought about their suffering and their situation in every step he took on the way to Calvary. Jesus identifies completely with the poor and rejected. Although poor, she wants to send her buggy, if she had one, to fetch Jesus. She reminds me of a Black mother who always wants to give her best to those who suffer. Nothing was too good for her to give to Jesus. When one sees Christ in the stranger or friend, one is willing to identify with Christ's suffering, and to offer Christ the best one has. This means that the friend or stranger may not be excluded or marginalized, but affirmed and valued in community.

It is an interesting exercise to reflect on the role Jesus plays in the community of the oppressed. In the church I attend, we speak of Jesus as "the way maker," and it does not matter how difficult the circumstances are, the faith of the "saints" is anchored in "Christ being in our midst." But it is important to note that faith for the saints is not information or a set of skills, but a relationship with Christ. Because of this, the saints can sing "Jesus is a shelter in the time of storm," or "Christ is our hope for years to come." The bottom line is that our confidence and trust is in Christ. Faith in Christ also conjures up images of faithfulness. We have faith in the faithfulness of Christ. Christ is trustworthy and we are confident Christ will be faithful even when we are unfaithful. In a church in which we seek to be Christ to each other, we hold each other to very high standards. Because Christ does not disappoint us, ultimately, the church places faith in God. It is interesting that the woman who prays to Jesus thanks him that he is not like Massa Linkum who is too high to attend her church. Jesus takes time for poor Ethiopian women. The faithfulness of Jesus elicits her loyalty to the Christ she meets in the community.

There is in the Black church an obligation to be Christ to each other. The parable in Matt.25:40 is an interpretive key for understanding the solidarity of Jesus with the oppressed community. "In as much as you have done it unto one of the least of these my brethren, you have done it unto me." The Black church survived because of the gifts of faith expressed as faithfulness, trust in Christ, and a sense of hope that Jesus would never forsake the community. At times when the church failed to practice faith in each other and in Jesus there was suspicion and the loss of confidence in a common future. Penalties were often very harsh when it was discovered that a member of the community, because of "bad faith," betrayed the values that hold the community together. In these times of distrust the community looks beyond itself to the one who constitutes its essence, Jesus. In these times the church sings, "Jesus is a rock in a weary land," or "Jesus has never failed me yet." It is the faithfulness of Jesus that holds the church together and allows Black people to hold body and soul together even in the face of betrayal and profound disappointment.

It was this faith in God as the one who is fair and faithful that made members of the Black church insist on reading the Bible for themselves and interpreting the scriptures in terms of racial uplift and dissatisfaction with the oppressive conditions under which they lived. Martin Delaney writing in 1852 places the issue before us:

> We are no longer slaves, believing any interpretation that our oppressors may give the word of God, for the purpose of deluding us to the more easy subjugation; but free men, comprising some of the first minds of intelligence and rudimental qualifications, in the country. What then is the remedy, for our degradation and oppression? This appears now to be the only remaining question—the means of successful elevation in this our native land.[4]

According to Delaney the people of God cannot exist meaningfully in terms of their own elevation as a people unless they practice faith in relation to each other and claim their ability to interpret the Word of God for themselves. One of the marks of freedom is to trust the members of your community, those who are bonded with you in the search for dignity and in the determination to foster the elevation of the race. Delaney offers a hermeneutic for a meaningful interpretation of the Word of God. The first principle is that the Bible is the community's book, and the Black community needs the confidence to interpret this book for themselves. It is the community's reading of the text that is important. And the community should not give this privilege and responsibility to those who are invested in the "degradation and oppression" of the community. For Delaney, the community needs to hear directly from God through members of the community in whom there is trust and fidelity. There is a correlation between the Biblical text and the contemporary context. The veracity and authenticity of the Word has to be tested in the situation in which the people hope for a better life and struggle to survive. The bottom line is the church cannot accept as authentic a Word from God that comes through a hierarchal leader.

Of course Delaney is responding to the fear Black people have of the White interpretation of the scriptures. The White interpretation of the scripture was almost always linked to a political agenda. The Bible was often used to justify oppression and the status quo. The Bible was often used to keep Black people in their place. Albert Raboteau gives an illustration of the kind of sermon Black people would hear from the White preacher during slavery:

> You slaves will go to heaven if you are good, but don't ever think that you will be close to your mistress and master. No! No! There will be a wall between you; but there will be holes in it that will permit you to look out and see your mistress when she passes by. If you want to sit behind this wall, you must do the language of the text "Obey your masters."[5]

According to Raboteau the Black community often complained that when they went to church the White master was standing there to ensure that the White preacher did his bidding and taught submissiveness. Many sermons instructed slaves not to lie or steal from old master and that they should obey the master under all conditions. "The preacher came and...He'd just say, 'Serve your masters. Don't steal your master's turkey. Don't steal your master's chickens. Don't steal your master's hawgs. Don't steal your master's meat. Do whatsomeever your master tells you to do."[6] It is no wonder that Delaney, writing some time later, would counsel the community to recognize that the Bible is the community's book, and that they are required to read the Bible in the light of the elevation of the race, spurning all who made themselves oppressors by interpreting the scriptures to keep intact structures of degradation and humiliation. Delaney seems to suggest a principle of correlation between the Biblical Word and the existential situation. The Word should be responsive to the needs of the community, and interpreters of texts should be careful not to represent the interests of the status quo. Biblical interpretation that is faithful to the need for liberation in the community should not betray the interests of the community. Slave preachers were known to break faith with the community and parrot the wishes of the master in their sermons because of fear of reprisals if they preached the Word of God as they understood it.

Questions raised here are pertinent for pedagogy in classroom and in ecclesial contexts. Whose interests are represented in the selection of and interpretation of texts? In what sense if any are the texts used for the empowerment and edification of the community and not primarily to maintain an institutional ethos? In the language of Martin Delaney, is the choice of and interpretation of texts for the elevation of the community? The central issue has to do with the meaning of education. Is education for liberation or for keeping things the way they are?

Other Black theologians of the nineteenth and twentieth centuries, such as Bishop Henry McNeil Turner and Marcus Garvey, further serve to remind us that the roots of Black theology are in the Black church. The concept of the Blackness of God, which appeared in Black theology in the 1960s and 1970s, was being discussed more than a century earlier in the Black church. Bishop Henry McNeil Turner who was elected bishop of the African Methodist Church in 1880 took Martin Delaney seriously as he read the Bible in the light of the Black experience, and indicated that on the basis of his reading, he could affirm that God is Black. Turner wrote:

> We have as much right biblically and otherwise to believe that God is a Negro, as you buckra or white people have to believe that God is a fine looking, symmetrical and ornamented white man. For the bulk of you and all the fool Negroes of the country believe that God is white-skinned, blue eyed, straight haired, projected nose, compressed lipped and finely robed white gentleman, sitting upon a throne somewhere in the heavens. Every race of people since time began who have attempted to define their god by words, or by paintings or carvings, or any other form of figure, have conveyed the idea that the God who made them and shaped their destinies was symbolized in themselves, and why should not the Negro believe that he resembles God as much as other people?...we certainly protest against God being white at all.[7]

Turner was the preeminent Black liberation theologian at the turn of the century. Convinced that White America would not treat Black people fairly, he advocated the return of Black people to Africa. His dream was to open up a way between the United States and Africa for the evangelization of Africa. Turner believed that White people in America had engendered the displeasure of God because of the way they had treated Black people in refusing to accept Black people as equals, and because of their unwillingness to share resources with their less privileged compatriots. It was his dream that African Americans from within the church would establish a Black nation in Africa free from European imperialism and White rule in the United States. In this vein, he saw the Black approach to religion as protest against the White church, whose exclusionary practices resulted in low self-esteem and notions of inferiority among Black church people. Turner's articulation of a Black God, the insistence that Black people would see God within the context of the Black experience, was a reversal of the values that breed inferiority among the Black community. The Blackness of God ensures the sanctity and dignity of the Black community. The ultimate signifier of Black people's alienation from Africa and the values of the Black community is the embrace of a White God. The freedom to talk about God from within the context of the Black community meant that they could define and interpret their own reality in terms of Blackness.

Closely related to the Black liberation theology espoused by Bishop Turner was Marcus Garvey, a contemporary of Turner. As founder of the Back to Africa movement, he envisioned the return of Africans in the Diaspora to their homeland. Africans in the Diaspora were captives in the White man's land, and Garvey was convinced that it was God's will for them to return to the land of their ancestors. His vision for people of African descent everywhere was racial pride, race consciousness, and material and educational attainments. This provided a basis for the motto of the organization he led: "One God! One Aim! One Destiny!" Garvey uses theological language to challenge social inequality in the African Diaspora. His message of racial pride and self-esteem, and his interpretation of everything including God, through the lens of Africa, were poignant. Garvey puts it this way:

> If the white man has the idea of a white God, let him worship his God as he desires. If the yellow man's God is of his race let him worship his God as he sees fit. We, as Negroes, have found a new ideal. Whilst our God has no color, yet it is human to see everything through one's

spectacles, and since the white people have seen their God through white spectacles, we have only now started out (late though it be) to see our God through our own spectacles. The God of Isaac and the God of Jacob let Him exist for the race that believes in the God of Isaac and the God of Jacob. We Negroes believe in the God of Ethiopia....We shall worship him through the spectacles of Ethiopia.[8]

Garvey's insistence on Africa as an organizing principle and the importance of seeing God through the lens of Africa were important keys in the formation and articulation of Black theology.

Garvey was fired by the spirit of Black nationalism, which pushed him to ask questions such as: "Where are Black people's factories to provide employment for their people? Why should Black people always walk hat in hand begging white people for jobs?" In response to these questions, Garvey formulated the aims and objectives of his movement: "To establish a Universal Confraternity among the race; to promote the spirit of pride and love; to reclaim the fallen; to administer to and assist the needy; to assist in civilizing the tribes of Africa; to assist in the development of independent Negro communities; to establish a central nation for the race, where they will be given the opportunity to develop themselves;...to establish Universities, Colleges, Academies and schools for racial education and culture of the people; to improve the general condition of Negroes everywhere."[9] With these goals and objectives informing his Universal Negro Improvement Association (UNIA) coupled with his untiring work for racial uplift, both in Jamaica and later in Harlem, New York, it should not surprise us that Garvey founded a church, the African Orthodox Church (AOC), with the help of Bishop George Alexander McGuire, who served as chaplain general of the UNIA.

McGuire, who hailed from St. Thomas in the Virgin Islands, had roots in the Moravian Church, and later became affiliated with the Episcopal Church while in New York and Philadelphia. The AOC became the official church of the UNIA. While members of the UNIA were not required to join, they were expected to if they did not have a church home.

The AOC was strongly West Indian....It maintained fraternal relations with the Russian Orthodox Church and when the General Synod of the Independent Episcopal Church met to become the African Orthodox Church, an unsuccessful move was made to omit "African" from its name and substitute "Holy." The AOC admitted persons of all races but according to its Constitution it "particularly sought to reach

out and enfold the millions of African descent in both hemispheres."
At the ... Fourth International Convention ... McGuire advised Negroes
to name the day when all members of the race would tear down and
burn any pictures of the white Madonna and Child and replace it with
a Black Madonna and Child.[10]

At the fourth convention of the UNIA in New York City in 1924, the
question concerning the color of God came to the floor. Garvey's
theological position was affirmed that God is spirit with the proviso
that Black people should nonetheless visualize God in their image and
likeness. "Remarked an old lady from Alabama, 'No white man
would die on the cross for me.' A delegate from Mississippi said, 'The
man of sorrows ain't nothing else but a colored man,' to which many
said, 'Amen, brother.'"[11] The *New York Journal* reported: "Marcus
Garvey, President-General of the Universal Negro Improvement
Association offers one reasonable suggestion. He says, 'God tells us to
worship him in our own image. We are Black, and to be in our image
God must be Black. He insists, therefore, on a Black God for colored
people, with Black saints, and in addition demands the whole of
Africa for the colored race.'"[12]

One could argue that Garvey's rhetorical skills were at work, and
that by insisting each race view God in its own image and likeness,
he left the door open for God to be or to become Black. He contended that God was spirit, and therefore transcended race, but at
the same time he asserted that God is race specific, as Black people
have no choice but to visualize a Black God. The founding of his own
church was Garvey's way of institutionalizing his ideas about God.
He understood better than most people the indissoluble connection
between religion and societal values. The way to shape beliefs in the
Black community is to keep in mind that Black people are "incurably
religious." Religion and religious values suffuse all of life.

The importance for our study of turning to Bishop Henry McNeil
Turner and to Marcus Garvey is to note their struggle at the turn of
the twentieth century with issues of self-esteem and dignity and the
way in which they responded to these issues by relating God to the
critical question of color that defined the community. Although Black
theology in its present form became widely recognized through the
writings of James Cone and J. Deotis Roberts, it must not be thought
that this theology began in the 1960s or 1970s; rather, its roots are in
the attempts of generations of Black people to understand themselves
and their environment from a Christian perspective. In the period of

slavery, these roots are in folklore, sermons, songs, and speeches. The raw material would not be formal theological reflection but, similar to the Hebrew Scriptures, God's history with God's people in struggle. To affirm this connection between Israel and Black people is to begin to understand that the Black church was both cradle and context of Black people's attempt to understand their world and themselves.

Turner and Garvey remind us that when Black theology is read in the light of God joining Black people in their struggle to transform oppressive institutions, the possibility of the new breaks through. Black people began to draw conclusions that God meant freedom for them, and that this God works with them in securing their freedom. This gave confidence to Turner and Garvey as they argued persuasively that Black people, like the children of Israel, were captives in the White man's land, and it was God's will that they be set free. Both leaders in the Black community devoted their lives to the explication of Black pride and Black dignity in the community. Following in the footsteps of Delaney, Turner and Garvey maintained that there was no need for Black people to read the scriptures in the light of a White ideal. To interpret the Black community in the light of a White ideal was to foster alienation of Black people from their best selves. This was the onto-logical problem that Turner and Garvey addressed—that to see God as White is for Black people to interpret their reality in the light of a White ideal. This perspective is certain to foster low self-esteem and negative feelings about a Black self or Black community. With Turner and Garvey insisting on an incarnational theology in which God is seen through the lens of the Black experience, God is liberated from Whiteness and is set free to become Black. Garvey's background in the Methodist church in Jamaica would not allow him to speak of God as Black, except through the lens of the Black experience, as he struggled with the transcendence of God in a way that would make God acces-sible to other peoples. Both Garvey and Turner held out the hope of the transcendence of God for God to be what communities needed God to become. The important issue is that God, as presented from a Christian frame of reference, can begin to spell liberation for Black people because God identifies with their condition and their situation. Turner admon-ishes his people: "God is a Negro." And citing Psalm 68:31, Garvey could counsel his people that the hand of God was outstretched to save Ethiopia and Africans in the Diaspora.

Both Turner and Garvey illustrate what happens when the Black community is willing to read scripture from the perspective of its own experience, and not allow others to interpret scripture or the symbols of faith for the community. Their approach calls attention to the experiential model that is crucial for the repairing of the self and the restoration of pride and dignity in the Black community. This approach breaks the power of Whiteness as Blackness becomes the symbol of liberation and genuine humanity. In a world in which White skin meant social privilege and advantage and Black skin meant inferiority, to posit the Blackness of God was a way of imbuing Blackness with divinity. This is what faith in the providence of God must mean—that the power of Whiteness has been broken and that themes of protest and identity formation are the main keys in which Black theology is set. As Black church theology becomes experiential theology, with God being seen in the light of the Black experience, the Black community begins to say, "No!" to all that would deny them the right to affirm the humanity of the Black community.

As faith in God is related to the Black experience, Black theologians point up and point out that faith means freedom from the false estimate of the self as inferior to other selves. Faith as it is practiced in the community means that the order of injustice is passing away and God's new realm of self-acceptance and justice is breaking in. There is some basis when many Black churches enjoin the membership to act on their faith in God, meaning that faith is praxis. The claim is that parishioners are asked to practice faith: faith that is not conjoined with praxis is dead. This is what faith in God must mean in the present context of oppression: "that the old order changeth yielding place to new"—the old order in which Black people would interpret community values in the light of White ideals.

In a world in which the White church often calls people to its ways, rather than to the ways of God, Black theology is the Black community's voice of protest against White supremacy and against the attempts of White people to play God in the area of race relations. In this regard, liberation is shouting that exploitation and victimization do not have their foundation in God's will, but in the attempt of oppressors to pretend that they are God. Black theology's exposure of the sin of racism exposed it for what it is: the very basis of sin in that it constitutes the attempt of people to deceive themselves by pretending they are God. In protest against this idolatrous use of skin color, Black theologians reversed categories and referred to Whiteness as evil, and to Blackness as the point of departure for talk about God, self, and world from the perspective of the Black church. One of the values of this form of protest and reversal of the categories, Whiteness and Blackness, is that it forces White people to clarify for themselves what they mean by

Whiteness. In the cruel world of oppression, Whiteness has always symbolized exploitation and dehumanization for the Black community. But because the Black church understands itself from the perspective of the divine revealed in their community, not only are they able to say no to the forces that impinge on its life in a negative way, but they are able to say yes to the divine activity within the community. With the Blessed Virgin Mary the Black church can say in Luke 1: 46–49, 51–53:

> My soul exalts the Lord, And my spirit has rejoiced in God my savior.
>
> For he has regard for the humble state of his bondslave; For behold, from this time all generations will count me blessed. For the Mighty One has done great things for me; And holy is his name....
>
> He has done mighty deeds with his arm; He has scattered those who were proud in the thoughts of their hearts. He has brought down rulers from their thrones, And exalted those who were humble. He has filled the hungry with good things; And sent away the rich empty-handed.[13]

Directions for the way forward in Black theology must come from the Black church. Not only must the community take time to express a resounding no to forces that encroach on the practice of freedom, but must also say yes to the presence of divine activity in its midst.

Wherever the divine presence is at work, people are being set free to identify themselves as children of dignity. We must enquire about the locus of divine activity in our midst. We must ask: What is God up to among us? The presence of the divine among us seen in our experience of Blackness would give us theological basis for talk about Black empowerment. As oppressed persons begin to transform situations of suffering into expressions of faith marked by the confidence of the divine to overcome oppressive situations, they begin to construct a new future, a new reality. Oppressed persons begin to learn that they were made for freedom, their vocation, calling, is to the construction of freedom. This construction of a new future and a new reality is marked by a robust refusal to be submissive in the face of suffering. Suffering and oppression do not have the last word. The decisive word belongs to the divine activity evidenced in the community's reaching and pressing toward the prize of freedom. The construction takes place in the midst of suffering as the oppressed carve out their new reality. It robs suffering of ultimacy, and gives ultimacy to freedom, even if it is snatched out of the jaws of suffering.

At this level, the community would be encouraged to reflect on the relationship between divine power and Black power. To ask about the divine activity in the Black community joins the discussion of the relationship between divine power and Black power. If Black power is defined as the search for self-determination, dignity, and freedom, then Black power is rooted in divine power. As divine power is related to Black power, oppressed people throw off the shackles of their oppression and join God in the work of liberation. As divine power is related to Black power, attention is called to the liberating content of faith and the social context in which this takes place. The liberating content of our faith announces that we are made in the image of God, the image of Blackness. This means that Blackness is not something to be avoided and rejected, but rather to be embraced and affirmed. The Blackness of God presents us with a new center of value in the community. Because God is Black, we do not have to hate anything associated with Blackness, but rather we begin to value and to affirm Blackness as the gift of divine presence. God has exalted those of low estate and the mighty God has thrown from their thrones. Because Blackness is the new center of value, we do not have to quest for the ideal self that was often beyond reach and forced us to hate the Black self.

I believe the consistent rise in "Black on Black" crime that afflicts the community has to do with the negative valuing of the self. The history of slavery and Jim and Jane Crowism has left the community despising and rejecting Blackness, and because of this self-hate, members of the community who see themselves in the mirror of the community seek to destroy what they see and hate. It makes a profound difference to have a different center from which to value self: the image of the divine in the community. The failure to accept Blackness as an organizing principle for the interpretation of God, world, and self is to accept Black self-hatred. The failure to value the Black religious experience as a frame of reference for understanding self-world is to begin to accept other people's stories as normative. It is a truism in the Black community that we cannot liberate ourselves with other people's stories. Failure to value our own stories and heritage fans the fires of Black self-hatred. Without access to one's story of survival and a sense of one's culture and heritage in a hostile environment is a recipe for self-destruction. Historically, this has been one of the gifts of the Black church to the community: that of helping the community understand how Black power—the community's search for self-determination and freedom—is related to the grace of God as this is mediated through the community. It is in this sense that the Black church has served as a source of refuge in a hostile environment for the Black community. Although Black people were denied participation in the social and economic life of mainstream America, and were often not accepted in White institutions of higher education, the church provided a creative context in which political power and justice were the right of members of the community. It was the theological commitment to justice, love, and empowerment of the oppressed that uniquely equipped the Black church to become the house of refuge for the Black community in its long march toward freedom and equality. The Black church became the Black sacred space in which weary travelers knew that the Almighty God was committed to their struggle for equality and dignity and victory was assured if they would endure to the end.

It is no secret that the Black community turned to the Black church not only for spiritual sustenance in its hymns, prayers, and sermons, but also for social and political support and leadership. The Black church proved to be a primary organizational resource in 1955, when Rosa Parks refused to relinquish her seat in the front of a bus in Montgomery, Alabama. Confronting the victimization of a Black family member and the need for the Black community to unify, Martin Luther King, Jr., was able to fill the breach with the help of the Black church. It was not his reading of the writings of the social gospel theologian Walter Rauschenbusch that provided the basis for his understanding that the task of the Black church was to redeem the soul of the community. In fact, it was his life in the community, as well as the demands the community made on the church, that made this obvious. The Black church's efforts to take the teachings of Jesus seriously made it imperative that the church reach out and redeem the soul of all of America. King states the issue for us:

> From the beginning a basic philosophy guided the movement. This guiding principle has been referred to variously as nonviolent resistance, noncooperation, and passive resistance. But in the first days of the protest none of these expressions was mentioned; the phrase most often heard was "Christian love." It was the Sermon on the Mount, rather than the doctrine of passive resistance, that initially inspired the Negroes of Montgomery to dignified social action. It was Jesus of Nazareth that stirred the Negroes to protest with the creative weapon of love.[14]

It is clear that redeeming the soul of America hinged on the practice of love for each other. At the heart of the Black church's understanding of love was the practice of gratitude and faithfulness among members of the household of God. Gratitude that the divine companions us in this journey called life. Gratitude for the divine presence in our midst and the assurance that the divine will be with us to the end of the journey.

But love reveals a commitment to faithfulness, the promise to be with each other and to be there for each other in the struggle for the soul of the community, and the soul of America. It means that this love of Christ that suffuses the life of the church joins those who are here in our immediate community, and those who are there outside the immediate context of the Black church. The practice of the love of God joins here and there, immanence and transcendence, those of the same kin, race, and religion with others who are different. It is in this sense that the Black church at its best has always been inclusive, always inviting the community and others to practice the love of God.

In addition to providing organizational leadership in the Black community, the Black church was also an important resource in economic leadership. The Black church has had a long history of pooling its resources to purchase lands and erect churches. In the time of Richard Allen and Absalom Jones, for example, the Black church in America promoted the organization of sickness and burial societies to provide support for dependents in times of catastrophic illness or death of the household breadwinner. Later, the Black church organized credit unions and benevolent societies to provide for the community's day-to-day financial needs. There were even some congregations that began their association as benevolent societies whose affiliate purpose was sustaining people materially as well as spiritually.

In the Black church tradition, issues of economics are often brought from the periphery to the center of theological attention. In this way the Black church often reminds us that Christianity is not merely a belief system but protest against poverty and forms of oppression that denude the human spirit. The Black church has always attached special significance to our Lord's mission statement in Luke 4:18–19, "The spirit of the Lord is upon me, because he hath anointed me to preach the gospel to the poor; he hath sent me to heal the broken hearted, to preach deliverance to captives, and recovering of sight to the blind, to set at liberty them that are bruised, to preach the acceptable year of the Lord."

The Black church taught that the surest way out of economic marginalization was education. Because of this, the Black church has always been a leader in providing educational institutions for the community. Lawrence Jones sums up the church's contribution:

> The churches' historic concern for education initially focused on efforts to compensate for the exclusion of Blacks from access to elementary education. After emancipation, the most pressing concern became that

of establishing and supporting secondary schools and colleges. By 1900 the churches had compiled an impressive record; Black Baptist associations were supporting some 80 elementary schools and 18 academies and colleges; the African Methodist Episcopal Churches were underwriting 32 secondary and collegiate institutions; and the smaller AME Zion denomination was supporting eight. The denomination now names the Christian Methodist Episcopal church, only 30 years old in 1900, had established five schools.[15]

Jones goes on to point out that the Black church has lost many of its gains in education today. In the wake of integration and as African Americans gain access to White schools, the need for Black-run and Black-owned schools have lessened. Accordingly, because of this many have closed and others struggle to attract the best teachers and administrators.

In a 2007 interview on CNN, comedian Bill Cosby pointed out that it costs about $8,000 to send a child to school for a year, and about $32,000 to incarcerate a person for a year. With close to one million persons of color in the penal system, who are either on parole, awaiting trial, or in jail, Cosby wonders where is the national will to invest more in the education of people of color. It seems to me that in this context, the Black church can play a crucial role once again to reawaken Black America's passion for learning. Our challenge is to reawaken the spirit of excellence and whet the appetite for learning. The Black church is uniquely poised to make this contribution. Perhaps a part of the challenge is to invest in Black youth, rather than these massive church buildings that seek to glorify the pastor. There are Black pastors who now boast that they have their own airplanes. We need to reprioritize and put people first, rather than the acquisition of material things. The challenge is to care enough to do everything to change the circumstances that thwart the lives of young people. It will take the community in its many forms to save the youth of our land. The Black church must provide the leadership.

The Black Church Faces the Future

Lawrence Jones notes that as the Black church faces the future, its existence is not in jeopardy, as the church will continue to be the only accessible institution where many people can find identity and belonging, both in the human and divine realm. He spells out a number of challenges the church must face as it confronts the future. As Jones sees it, the most pressing is for the church to become bilingual. The church must understand the language of the world and at the same time be able to translate the gospel into the idioms and symbols of that language. The church is required to mount programs that will address the realities of urban life for the masses of poor Black people. In the context of urban centers, we are reminded of systemic evils such as poverty, poor or nonexistent health care, and a justice system that often does not work in the interest of the poor. Churches will need to pool resources as they seek to affect the lives of people in urban centers. If Black churches in any given city would place their income in a single bank, it would provide tremendous leverage for influencing this bank's lending policy, especially in regard to urban neighborhoods. Jones presses for churches to buy goods together, save together, and cooperate in tackling the stubborn problems in the community.

Jones is also concerned that churches pay attention to the new self-identity in many Third World countries. "What does the indigenization of churches mean for black missionaries in black countries? Black church mission early reflected the 'redemption of Africa' theme. What does the term connote at a time when cultural Christianity is undergoing rigorous scrutiny? What does it mean to affirm indigenous religion while proclaiming the gospel of Jesus Christ? In the light of Third World realities, have the terms 'missions' and 'missionary' become anachronistic?"[16]

It is important to note that Jones' article was written in 1979, and it is interesting to highlight what was not mentioned in his projection for the future of the Black church. Although Black women comprise a majority in most congregations and the clergy is predominantly male, it is instructive that the issue of patriarchy and the absence of women from pulpits in these churches are void in Jones' work in 1979. He provides an important index for us in understanding the way in which the theology of the church in its language could exclude women. Jones would agree that the church in the 1970s could not survive without women, yet the church in much of its language concerning its identity and its future excluded women.

I would like to turn now to the article, "The Future of the Black Church," written by pastor Charles Spivey Jr., in 1983. Spivey speaks of his contribution from within the Black church with the hope of effecting radical change in that church. According to Spivey, the primary task of the Black church as it faces the future is to understand itself as a faithful community that remembers, recalls, and reminds Black people of their heritage. The Black church must function as the memory of the Black community. "Our history cannot be entrusted to the hands of those who have not lived it.... Who will keep alive the history of auction blocks, chains, whips, and branding? The terror and danger of slaves who ran away? The struggle to survive in northern cities.... Jews remember Auschwitz not to keep hatred for Germans alive, but to keep themselves aware, alert AND ALIVE."[17] Neither Blacks nor Jews should forget their history of suffering.

If the first task of the Black church as it faces the future is to remember its past and celebrate its heritage, the second is the formation of nurturing communities in which Black people may find hope and direction. This is crucial for two reasons: 1) the reality of racism and 2) the high incidence of crime of Blacks against Blacks. While racism is a fact of American life that Black people may lack the power to change, its consequence of Black on Black crime demands immediate attention from the church.

> The Black church cannot fulfill its mission and ignore the high incidence of crime perpetuated by Blacks against Blacks; or that homicide is the third highest cause of death among Black males between 16 and 25 years of age; or the alarming increase in suicide rate among young Blacks, male and female; or overlook the fact that actual violence against children, women, and senior citizens far exceeds the actual cases reported.[18]

Because the Black church embraces an ethic of care as an important part of its future plan for the community, it must give particular attention to formation of youth. "Black churches, once the education center in the formation of moral and ethical values and attitudes, seem now to be as much the victim as other institutions of the powerful influence of models and standards imposed from outside the community."[19] The Black church must encourage families to become involved in the lives of young people. Spivey laments that there was a time in the Black community when Black families were proactive concerning the education of young people. Black churches must provide leadership in assisting families to combine education and nurture for youth at risk.

Priorities for the future are clear if the Black church is to become source and resource for a new quality of life in the Black community. The church must help the community remember and recall its history and heritage of suffering. Spivey seems to suggest that the appropriate starting place for planning a new future in the Black community is the cross of suffering, which points to the possibility of transformation as Black people participate in creating communities of nurture and hope. Spivey seems to struggle with the question of how one moves from this negative history of suffering and exploitation to one of hope and nurture. It is precisely at this point he seems to indicate that the Black community must enter into the situation of suffering, and not merely submit to it, but aim to transform it. It is the struggle of Black hope in the present that offers the possibility of a new future.

Under the rubric of nurture as an important ingredient in the formation of Black community, sexism appears as a blimp on Spivey's radar screen. This is a significant accomplishment for Black theologians in 1983. In the *Chicago Theological Register*, which was dedicated to addresses by four eminent Black theologians, Spivey was the only one who spoke to the issue of sexism, and he did this in three paragraphs. Spivey notes that the Black church is guilty of using the Epistles of Paul to keep Black women in their "place." The challenge at hand is to eradicate sexism in the church, as it hinders the emergence of a vital and compassionate community. The central issue is not just the question of leadership in ecclesial communities, but the facilitating of a new style of relationship between men and women that will allow a healthy, vital, and nurturing community to emerge. Spivey does not provide any strategies as to how this new community will emerge, but he is saddened that the matter of sexism is barely discussed in the church.

The mood changes when we get to the 1990s as C. Eric Lincoln and Lawrence H. Mamiya devote a chapter in their book, *The Black Church in the African American Experience*, to "The Black Church and Women." They remind us that in the major Black denominations, the membership is predominantly women who hold key positions in these churches. "Women serve in myriad roles in black churches as evangelists, missionaries, stewardesses, deaconesses, lay readers, writers on religious subjects, Sunday School teachers,...and directors of vacation Bible School."[20] We are told that women wield power in the church, in part because of their numbers, but also through honorific positions such as "mothers of the church," which is often reserved for the oldest female member or the wife of the founder. It is not unusual for the pastor to consult the church mother when important decisions are to be made. Often, it is not very helpful for the pastor if the church mother disagrees with his position.

In spite of the sheer force of numbers and the many offices that are held by women, in the Black church the office of minister and pastor is largely reserved for a male. Lincoln and Mayima indicate that the root of this tradition of male preachers and pastors is a relic from White Christianity as it was presented to enslaved and free Black persons throughout the United States. One of the main gospel lessons taught by the White preacher was "wives obey your husbands, slaves obey your masters." The main theme in which the gospel was set was submissiveness.

What is interesting is that it did not have to be this way because the ways in which Black people were socialized in West Africa was one in which women were leaders in the community. In the African context, "women were priestesses, queens, midwives, diviners, and herbalists; they were among the major practitioners of good and evil witchcraft. There were also female deities in the complex cosmology of different ethnic groups."[21] In the expressions of African religions that can be seen throughout the Caribbean, women are often leaders in the religious rituals. This was often true also in the United States, especially in the practice of Voudou, and the dispensing of herbal medicine. But there was a difference in attaining the role of pastor or minister in the Christian church. One problem was that all the role models who preached this gospel were men and then one had to experience a call within the Protestant tradition to which most Black churches belonged, and this call usually had to be culturally endorsed and verified. Women had to squelch the call to become pastors, as this was often culturally unacceptable. The dominant culture defined the parameters of women's calling and work:

> American society considered the slave woman primarily as a source of cheap labor and as a breeder, the instrument by which the slave status would be passed on "durante vita," from generation to generation and the supply of slaves could be ensured indefinitely. The patriarchal values of the larger society and of Christianity itself added the burden of sexism, including sexual exclusion from the vocation of ministry.[22]

When Black people were able to administer their own churches they adopted the rules and culture learned from White churches. They did not turn to African models for an alternative model of church. There were too many Biblical injunctions that placed the leadership of the pastoral ministry in the hands of men. In this regard, the Black church has been unimaginative as it took over the male patriarchal worldview and applied it to the church, and as we saw earlier, also in the development of its theology. The first real challenge from women came in 1809 from Jarena Lee who at the age of twenty-four experienced a call to preach and approached Richard Allen pastor of Bethel African Methodist Episcopal Church for a license to preach. "Although Allen could see women leading prayer meetings, he drew the theological line against female preaching and refused to issue the license requested. However, impelled by her call Jarena Lee preached without it."[23] This was the fate of many women during this period and throughout the history of the Black church who experienced the call to preach. Many women turned to teaching, or to social work as ways of dealing with this call.

The Black Church as Hope of Black Community

Earlier, we noted that Charles Spivey spoke of the Black church as memory of the Black community. We were reminded that the Black church has traditionally been very patriarchal, and it has been the main instrument of integrating the Black family into Western patriarchal values. Exceptions along these lines have been many Pentecostal and storefront churches in which women have served as leaders. I am unsure concerning the correlation between women who serve as heads of families usually in which the Black male is absent, and the leadership provided in these churches. The church, however, has served as conserver of the values of the community, especially as these relate to Black identity. In a racist society in which the Black male was treated as boy and relegated to the sphere of unimportance, the Black church provided public space for the Black male to exercise power. In this context, the pastor became the African chief, the patriarch of the community, and he was looked to as father for all the children in the community whose fathers were absent. It is a known fact that one of the evils of slavery was that of robbing the Black male of his right to be father to his family. The pastor became symbol of the one who would protect, provide, and pray for the Black community. Vicariously, he stood in the place of the missing father and the community bestowed on him all the virtue and pride for which they hoped. When I served as pastor of a Black church in Harlem, New York, there were many men in this church who claimed that the only place they had a chance to assert themselves as men was in the church. According to them, the church provided a context in which Black male pride was repaired and restored.

The good news was that men could give sociological concreteness to their hope for somebodiness, and work to realize this in the church. What was interesting in the church in which I served as pastor and subsequently in a church I pastored in Atlanta is that the women went along with this view of male empowerment at their expense. Women in these churches attributed to themselves the virtues of selflessness and sacrifice and argued that in a society in which the Black male is emasculated, a part of their responsibility is to make room for the restoration of the dignity and pride in the Black man. Their pride was derivative as the Black preacher represented them.

Of course the critical question that confronts us is: How may the Black church serve as source and resource of human flourishing for all of God's children, male and female? If the Black church is not only memory, but hope of the Black community, what may we remember and for what may we hope? It is appropriate to note that hope is more than optimism. In the Christian church we are accustomed to talk about the coming expectation of the realm of God. We hope for a new future, one we believe is discontinuous in many respects from the negative past of slavery and discrimination. In many Black churches we often associate hope with the expectation of newness of life. We dream of God breaking-in and doing something qualitatively new. Hope in God opens up a new future for us. It is a future marked by the freedom to dream, and the marking of the Black church as the community in which the dream of women serving in all areas of the church becomes a reality. Martin Luther King, Jr. taught us that we are made of dreams, and hope teaches us that we can live in the confidence that God will help us to change not only the course of our individual lives, but that of the church. As our hope for newness of life embraces the freedom to carry out lives that are pleasing to God, we exit traditions that dehumanize and thwart the promise of human flourishing.

No longer will we postpone our hope for a new future in which male and female are invited to serve in all areas of the church. We will not postpone this dream "to the sweet bye and bye," or "when we all get to heaven." Because our hope is confident we will begin to agitate in our churches as we alter the circumstances that seek to circumscribe hope. Our churches are experiencing a new surge of hope in God's faithfulness to help us create sacred space for us to live out our vocation to be human.

May we assert then that as the ethos of the Black church informs practice in the classroom, pedagogy becomes the construction of sacred space in which all of God's children are assured a new future?

A future that is discontinuous with a racist, sexist, classist, and homophobic past. A new future in which sacred spaces are provided for members of the class to become Christ to each other as hierarchy is discarded, as students teach and teachers learn. It is in this new space bracketed by a new future that new truths about us will emerge.

5

Emancipatory Praxis and Liberation
for Oppressors

In an important essay on the liberation of oppressors, Jurgen Moltmann claims it is a sin for one human being to oppress another as scripture stipulates that if we do not practice love for persons whom we have seen, it is impossible to love God whom we have not seen. I would like to look at the main outline of Moltmann's article for a number of reasons: 1) womanist theologians point out that although they have been oppressed by Black males who have excluded them in the articulation of Black theology, and in leadership positions throughout the Black church, because their theology represents the "politics of wholeness," Black men, indeed the entire Black family must be included and 2) womanist theologians, in their offer of liberation to oppressors, do not only cross barriers of gender, including the Black male, but racial barriers in including the White woman. Black women, as they construct a theology from their experience of exclusion in terms of gender and race, practice liberation for their oppressors, in part because in relation to White women, they are the outsiders who are within, and in relation to Black men they are the insiders who are often on the outside. Womanist theology may be the only expression of liberation theology that explicitly addresses and includes in its praxiological task the liberation of oppressors. Other expressions of liberation theology are focused primarily on the liberation of the oppressed. The question that womanist thinkers pose for us is: What if the liberation of the oppressed includes the oppressor?

I find it interesting that whether one looks at the articulation of womanist theology by Jacquelyn Grant, Linda Thomas, or Kelly Brown-Douglas, one sees a theology of inclusion for both Black and

White persons. The generative question for our investigation is: What does it mean for womanist theology to be the vehicle for the inclusion of the human family in the politics of wholeness? With womanist theologians we take as our point of departure the theological claim that it is only the oppressed who in liberating themselves can also offer liberation for oppressors, both Black and White.

Whether one views reality from the perspective of an oppressor or as an oppressed person, one is victimized. One way of looking at the matter is whether one is victimized by structures one has created, or one is the recipient of victimization. The oppressor participates in a system of oppression that diminishes and stultifies human life. The oppressor stands on the side of the master, on the other side of the oppressed person. The oppressed represent those who are subjugated, those who are not allowed to relate as subjects, but as objects; those whose voice has been stolen. Both the oppressor and the oppressed have lost their essential self and are estranged and alienated from their best selves. The oppressor's essential self is destroyed through evil: racism, sexism, classism, and homophobia. The essential self of those who are oppressed is destroyed through suffering, which often leads to despair and the loss of identity. Moltmann puts it this way:

> Oppression destroys humanity on both sides but in different ways: on the one side through evil, on the other through suffering. The evil of the one is the cause of the suffering of the other, and the latter is the consequence of the former. If oppression has these two aspects, then the process of *liberation* from oppression must begin simultaneously on both these sides: the liberation of the oppressed from suffering under oppression occurs simultaneously with the liberation of the oppressors from the sin of oppression, and vice versa. Otherwise there is no true liberation into freedom. The goal can be nothing other than the new and true communion of humankind, in which there are no longer either oppressed or oppressors.[1]

Something terrible happens in the process of becoming oppressor and oppressed. Both lose their essential beings as human; on the one hand as doers of evil, and on the other as objects of sufferings. What I find intriguing in Moltmann's theology for oppressors is the congruence between his analysis and that of womanist theologians who claim that the liberation of the oppressed occurs simultaneously with that of oppressors. The goal is what womanist thinkers call "the politics of wholeness," or the liberation of the human family, that includes both oppressed and oppressors.

Womanist thinkers are insistent that the liberation of the human family is at stake, and that part of what this means is Black women, who are the key to the liberatory process, are willing to provide leadership in crossing racial, gender, class, and homophobic barriers in order to save the soul of America. The crucial point for womanist theologians is that liberation must restore and repair the humanity of both oppressor and oppressed, and it does not really matter whether the oppressor is White or Black, they are included in the politics of wholeness. Moltmann notes that there are two distinct problems to consider in navigating the relationship between both. There is a moral component involved in the liberation of the oppressed, and there is a religious component involved in the liberation of the oppressor.

The oppressed are often victims of the indiscriminate use of power, they suffer innocently, and it is a moral duty for them to exit these relationships and traditions that stultify their being. Womanist thinkers indicate that there is a moral imperative to redeem humanity on both sides, and this becomes rather complicated as it is not usually apparent that both oppressor and oppressed need liberation. For example, in a classroom setting it is often easy to identify those who are mute, or those who feel that they are overwhelmed, and therefore have nothing to contribute. On the other hand, those who always seem to participate and often monopolize the class discussion often do not see their need for liberation from a sense of their own importance and their need to allow rhetorical space for the less articulate. What we need to be aware of as we explore an emancipatory pedagogy is that the contextual realities of oppressed and oppressors are different. While it is often easy and self-evident to see the need for the liberation of the oppressed, it is always more difficult for the oppressor to see the need for liberation. Moltmann argues that one reason for this inability to see their own danger is oppressors' focus on the advantages of their sin. They often benefit from a relationship of exploitation and the misuse of power. "Oppressors are for the most part blind: they do not see the suffering of their victims, which they have brought about. They justify their evil on many grounds; they are blinded."[2] Because the oppressed often see that liberation is in their own interest, there is a correlation between identifying the need for liberation and the seeking to overcome or overthrow the conditions that engender their oppression in the first place. In a profound sense the liberation process includes the desire and interest of the oppressed to be made whole or to be set free. This, Moltman contends, is not the case for oppressors. Because they benefit from a lifestyle that is oppressive to others, the advantage of sin blinds them from seeing the necessity for liberation. While the oppressed will see the need and express an interest and desire for liberation, the oppressor experiences a contradiction between the interests and desires of being an oppressor and the need for liberation. The reality of liberation is often not consonant with the interests and desires of the master class. We see this in the classroom or ecclesial context from time to time when men often seek to represent women or the more articulate seek to speak for the less articulate. This is also the case where we find an articulate teacher or student who is excellent at sharing his/her views, but has poor listening skills. It is often difficult to help the other see that learning to listen is in her/his interest and more importantly in the interest of the class.

It is precisely at this point that Moltmann, in agreement with womanist thinkers, argues that because of the nature of oppression and the capacity of the self to deceive itself, the liberation of oppressors is a religious, and not a moral task. Womanist thinkers contend that oppressors who are unable to see their faults are unable to liberate themselves. The challenge is not for oppressors to save themselves or to lift themselves by their own bootstraps. Liberation for oppressors has to be mediated, another has to make this possible, a Christ figure or others who will be there as agents of liberation.

It must be noted that in 1979, when Moltmann wrote this essay, womanist theology was in its embryonic form, and had not yet revolutionized ways of being and knowing among oppressed groups. In 1979, it would have been correct to say that liberation theologies were one-sided, in that they were only concerned for the liberation of oppressed groups. In this vein, Moltmann mentions the Exodus paradigm in which the oppressed Israelites struggle to leave Egypt for freedom. By contrast, the oppressors had to await the work of Christ in cross and resurrection. "For the liberation of the oppressed the biblical traditions contain the well-known and always inspiring tradition of Exodus. Through hope and struggle the oppressed enter on the way to freedom. By contrast, the liberation of oppressors comes about by means of the suffering and death of Christ on the Cross; it means the forgiveness of sins, repentance and rebirth to new life in discipleship to the Crucified."[3]

I find it interesting that Moltmann characterizes liberation theologies as theologies of Exodus and resurrection. This I do not believe is quite the case with Black and womanist theologies. It is true that the Exodus motif is central in these theologies as the oppressed are called on to exit traditions and circles of destruction that lead to death. The figure of Moses is a very popular one in Black ecclesiology and theologies, as Moses is often asked to "go tell old Pharoah to let God's people go." And yet, on the other side of liberation is new life, resurrection to the newness of life. Liberation is seen more often as a process, and full resurrection or reconciliation is seen as an eschatological possibility. But what Moltmann may have missed, especially in the case of Black theology—because when he wrote, womanist theology was in its infancy—is that the reality of Blackness, with which Christ identified completely, was the contemporary expression of the cross of Christ for the Black community. The oppressor is not without hope, provided he is willing to come through Christ, who takes on the form of the Black community. The theological and ethical imperative is that the liberation for the oppressed and the oppressor means coming through the door of Blackness. Unless one becomes Black—that is take on the Black condition—and enter into solidarity with the oppressed, one cannot enter the realm of God. The truth is that this call to Blackness is inseparable from the call to Christ. The challenge was not for the Black community to become more like Christ; the call was for Christ to become Black. Both Black and womanist theologies caught on to this need for an incarnational theology: they begin with the tragic, the grotesque, the contemporary cross, and womanist theologians inform us that it is the cross of Black womanhood with which Christ identifies that serves as symbol of hope and liberation for oppressors, both White and Black.

Liberation for Oppressors: Changing Power Relations

An important question for us is whether Moltmann is talking about something else, when he calls for the liberation of oppressors. Is he calling attention to the cross of Christ, which is independent of the Black condition? Is he appealing to the cross of Christ *extra nos*. It seems to me that what Moltmann may be up to in this text, and perhaps in his earlier work, *The Crucified God*, is to posit a way of talking about the cross of Christ that is not anchored in the Black experience of suffering. At stake for our discussion is the role of context in talk about emancipatory praxis. My sense is that Moltmann seeks to dislodge the cross of Christ from "the hermeneutical privilege of the oppressed" and place it in neutral ground where the oppressor may access the cross without reference to the oppressed. What he failed to see is that the cross of Christ is inseparable from the oppressed condition. This is the theological import of Matt. 25:35, "For I was hungry and you gave me food, I was thirsty and you gave me something to drink, I was a stranger and you welcomed me." The point that Moltman did not see in the American context is that the Black oppressed condition is inseparable from the cross through which all oppressors must come if they hope to experience forgiveness, practice repentance, and witness to new life made possible by the cross of Christ.

Moltmann points out that while he is sympathetic to notions of Black, feminist and different stripes of liberation theologies being theologies of Exodus and resurrection, as oppressed persons need to leave various contexts of oppression and claim resurrection, he is aware that at the same time these expressions of liberation theology are not theologies of cross and judgment. According to Moltmann, this theology—liberation theology—is inadequate because it does not address the need of the oppressor for liberation. "We may rightly criticize the fact that so far no theology of liberation has emerged on the other side of the oppressive situation. That we allow ourselves to be frightened or supported by the black, feminist, and socialist theologies of liberation, and have become tolerant and benevolent towards them, is a mark of callousness, not of intelligence. We need a 'liberating theology for oppressors.' "[4]

Moltmann has not pondered with sufficient depth the openness of Black theology and Black church practice of making room for the stranger, the person of another race, gender, and class. J. Deotis Roberts places the issue before us:

> Whites have ignored the requirements "of love, justice and mercy." They are guilty of malpractice as Christians; they have been hypocritical and involved in double-dealing in the area of race. Words and deeds have been antithetical. Dishonesty and indifference have been common among whites even in integrated congregations and denominational bodies. White Christians have been living and behaving thus in an inauthentic manner. Black Christians who have passively accepted the blunt end of the misinterpretation and malpractice of white Christians have also lived an inauthentic existence. It is the goal of a worthy Black Theology to lead both blacks and whites to an authentic Christian existence. The true life of faith should be for whites one that would enable them to accept all humans as equals to themselves. Black Christians are to be led to true self-understanding, self-respect, true manhood, and fulfillment as sons of God.[5]

Roberts' text was published in 1971, while Moltmann's article was published in 1979. It is quite clear from the pronouncements by Roberts that Black theology does not limit itself to an assessment of the existential plight of oppressed people, but sees its task as that of proffering reconciliation between Black and White people. This has been the theological posture of the majority of writers from the Black theology perspective. It is a carryover from the ethos of the Black church that embraces the stranger and alien. "Any black separatism, though arising directly from white resistance, must be understood as 'strategic withdrawal' for unity and empowerment, and not as permanent. Authentic existence for Blacks and whites can only be realized finally in reconciliation between equals in the body of Christ"[6] Roberts represents the orthodox position in Black and womanist theologies. The Christian is challenged to love all persons regardless of their social status, class, gender, or race. The position that Roberts articulates in 1971, as most theologians in the womanist and Black theology camp claim, that the existential cross that the Black community embraces necessitates the separation of the Black community from the White community as an emergency strategy in order to become spiritually powerful. The separation that Roberts advocates is a way of dealing with the need for a balance of power in order to come to the table of reconciliation. The precondition of reconciliation is liberation, and liberation means self-determination, the power to deliberate, and make decisions. According to Roberts, the separation of the Black community is a part of the strategy of liberation, and should not be considered as permanent, but as a necessary stage that precedes the breaking-in of the egalitarian realm of reconciliation.

The language of separation and reconciliation is another way of talking about cross and reconciliation. Moltmann, I contend, was mistaken in arguing that Black theology does not proffer a theology of the cross, but a theology of Exodus and resurrection. At the very center of Black theology is a struggle with the cross of the Black experience. It could be that the stumbling block for Moltmann concerns the mystery of the cross of Christ—that of seeing its inseparability from the Black experience. Faith in Christ is bearing the cross of Christ as the cross of the Black experience. Christ bore our punishment on his cross. To hate our cross is to hate his, and to love his cross is to love or own. In the final analysis, the cross of Christ is identical with our own. The cross is always the historical cross of Christ rooted in the Black experience.

Recently, I suggested to students in my class, who are two-thirds White and a third Black, that the cross of Christ is located in the poor Black community, and that for middle-class Black people and White people to "experience their own Easter" they will have to come through the poor Black community, where Christ identifies completely with the least of these. Both middle-class Black and White students claimed that the cross of Christ located outside the suburbs of Black middle-class and rich White communities would be irrelevant. Both groups of students asked: "Do you or Christ expect us to go *there* to the poor Black community?" "Why can't the cross be located in our community?" Then I questioned what repentance would mean if the cross of Christ was located in their middle-class and upper middle-class suburbs? What if our liberation is indissolubly linked with those edged outside our comfortable suburbs? One thing became clear for us: the cross as pedagogical resource meant that we had to linger with the questions; we could not rush to answers. Students wanted immediate resurrection; they did not want to talk about the implications of Saturday when Jesus remained in the tomb. We began to discover that we have to live with our questions and begin to learn that the answer is hidden in the question. The Christ who leads us out of traditions that are stultifying and demeaning is hidden in the cross of the poor.

Moltmann struggles with a theology for oppressors. He does not believe that the answer is hidden in the cross of Christ rooted in the community of the oppressed. He wants to look for liberation on the other side, in the community of oppressors. He puts it this way:

> Thus far we have arrived at no insights for a theology of oppressors from the theology of the oppressed. The reason for this is that we members of the white, masculine, rich world are indeed able to acknowledge the liberation of others, but are not willing to acknowledge ourselves as "oppressors." Thus we display good intentions but no insights. We want to be liberal and neglect thereby our liberation. Whoever wishes to help the oppressed to gain their freedom must begin with himself.[7]

Moltmann is self-consciously addressing himself to oppressors and complaining that they feel excluded and that they will have to anchor the cross of Christ not in the community of the oppressed but in a another context, perhaps in the community of oppressor, so that the oppressor may have access without having to relate to poor and marginalized persons. Oppressors are accustomed to have things their way and are in danger of manipulating the meaning of the cross. In fairness to oppressors, they taught Black people and people of color Christain theology, how then can they stand by and watch as the oppressed define the theological task?

But we should listen to Moltmann, not only because he raises afresh for us the question of the oppressor and the oppressed, which I suspect is true of most contexts in which persons seek to learn and teach, but because he provides clues in terms of what it means for oppressors to repent and to ask for forgiveness and to seek after newness of life. According to Moltmann, when one gets a glimpse of the cross of Christ, irrespective of the context in which one sees the cross, one begins to ask: "What's wrong with us?" and "How may we find our way?" We have been accustomed to hear oppressed persons talk about what is wrong and their existential need for liberation but now we hear from the other side. Moltmann clues us in concerning what is wrong with oppressors.

Exploring the Oppressor Within

Moltmann identifies the three cardinal sins of oppressors: racism, sexism, and capitalism. He shares with us the World Council of Churches definition of racism in 1968:

> By racism we mean ethnocentric *pride* in one's own racial group and preference for the distinctive characteristics of that group; belief that these characteristics are fundamentally biological in nature and are thus transmitted to succeeding generations; strong negative feelings towards other groups who do not share these characteristics coupled with the thrust to discriminate against and exclude the out group from full participation in the life of the community.[8]

A major problem with racism says Moltmann is the tendency to iden-tify the characteristics of one's group with what it means to be human; for example, to be human means to be White. The implication is that persons of other races do not measure up to what it means to be human. "The characteristics of one's own race are utilized for the purpose of self-justification. The feeling of self-value is based on one's own skin color. The right to domination is legitimated by one's own race: the northern or white races are destined to rule over 'mixed peoples' or 'slavish peoples' or 'underdeveloped peoples.' In racism one's own identity is always defined by means of discriminating against other races. For the racist identity is a negative, cramped, and aggressive identity."[9] Racism should not be confused with group egoism, which is present in many places but group egoism can become racist as pent up aggression seeks to express itself in terms of mastery and oppression, enslavement and exploitation of persons of other races. At this level racism does not manifest itself merely as a group phenomenon but as psychological warfare as a means of controlling the other. "Then persons of other races are banished to a lowly caste. As 'second class citizens' they are deprived of fundamental human and civil rights. As slaves and workers they are condemned to perpetual dependence. The superiority feelings of the dominant race engender feelings of inferiority in the subjugated class."[10]

Moltmann is most instructive for pedagogy in his counsel that while group egoism is everywhere, one needs to be on the alert as group egoism may lead to racist acts or ways in which the dominant group subjects other groups to subtle forms of exploitation, and in some cases reenforce an attitude of dependence. Another way in which the dominant group may communicate feelings of not being good enough is by setting low expectations for students who belong to subgroups. I have often had students from Third World countries complain of feeling demeaned by teachers who set the academic bar too low because they regard them as "less than" American students. Another way in which the superiority that American teachers often arrogate to themselves in relation to others from another culture is to "talk down" to them. It is often a way of asserting group egoism by appearing to come down to other groups. These are subtle forms of the superior inferior motif, but the point worth making is that the temptation to be an oppressor in the context of the classroom transcends race, as teachers and leaders in this context take on the characteristics of those who oppress from the vantage point of being a superior race. The dilemma with taking on the characteristics of a racist, in the context of the classroom, is that if one belongs to a race that is subjugated in the larger culture, one may not have the power to make these attitudes stick in the larger culture or even in the institution as a whole, since the institution is often run by people with the advantage of power. In many classrooms the professor/teacher has power to marginalize and to dehumanize.

This means that there are two levels at which those who teach and those who learn must look out for racist assumptions and their impact in the classroom. First, from those who by virtue of being members of the dominant society can use the privilege of this relationship to render persons of a different race powerless—people who are unable to tie into the racist assumptions implied in being and knowing in this context. This often expresses itself in the choice of texts. The assumption is that the only persons who have anything worth saying about the subject are White persons, therefore teachers insist on White sources in their students essays and term papers. But the risk of demeaning members of the class is true not only of persons who teach and belong to the dominant race, but also of those of us who have internalized the ways of the oppressor. There is a sense in which there is something of the oppressor in all of us and one of the places where this is expressed is in the classroom. The truth is that many of us who are Black and Latina/Latino still insist that the only texts worth reading in the humanities must be written by White males. This means that we have internalized a way of being and knowing that suggests that White male ways of knowing and being are superior to other ways. This semester I am teaching as an adjunct at a Black college where students who are all Black complain that they are required to prove that they are able to read and comprehend texts written by White authors as a way of showing that they can compete in the White world. They further complained that this practice was unfair to them, as White students at White colleges do not have to study Black texts in order to compete in a Black world.

We often call attention to this expression of White supremacy in the classroom when we see it practiced by White males and then overlook it in ourselves. Non-White teachers also have to guard against low expectations from non-White students and the tendency to talk down to them. It is precisely at this point Moltmann reminds us that there are two aspects to the practice of racism, an inner and an outer. Racism is a psychic mechanism for the self-justification and an ideological mechanism for the subjugation of persons who are different. The heart of the matter as Moltmann talks about it has to do with the role of the self and its relations with others. Racism is a way of justifying who we are in relation to the subjugation of others. It is a rather negative way of identifying self at the expense of others. Moltmann suggests that one way to overcome racism is not to self-identify as White (since he is addressing oppressors) but as human. The challenge is for White people to surrender their racist identity, and the second strategy to dismantle racism is a "redistribution of power" from the powerful to the powerless, and an openness to the creation of a new order in which new opportunities will exist for people to fashion a new humanity.

Moltmann would benefit greatly from a rereading of Black and womanist theologies as he seeks to posit ways to dismantle racism in the White world. His analysis, while helpful, is a little naïve as he has not talked about the ways in which the racism embedded in institutions provides structures for the practice of racism. It is rather difficult to travel on one set of tracks in the discussion of racism. One track is certainly the responsibility of the individual and an appropriate appeal for discipleship to the cross of Christ as a way of countering this force for evil. But when it is recalled that when Moltmann first presented this essay, it was at an American university, it is worth mentioning that matters of pedagogy could not be far away. His lecture was aimed at oppressors in the university context and his suggestion of ways to defeat racist practices was addressed to those who teach and learn in the university context. This was appropriate, but Moltmann did not address the corporate nature of sin, the ways in which institutional sin insinuates itself into the fabric and life of the school. Moltmann would have to ask the larger questions: What are the institutional policies and practices that keep intact a racist worldview? Who are the guardians of these policies? And what are the ways in which these practices and policies inform and influence the ethos of the university? An individual act of resistance, and confession, while important as signaling where the student or the teacher stands in relation to a racist culture, is inadequate as a means for dismantling racism. Are there strategies to be employed that begin to chip away at the institutional ethos?

In the discussion of racism, Moltmann has conversation partners with Black theologians who regard racism as the most urgent problem in America. The turn to sexism as a cardinal sin of oppressors joins the conversation with womanists and feminists who see sexism as even more insidious than racism in its ability and capacity to insinuate itself in institutions that seem on the surface to embrace an institutional ethos of justice and openness. Black and womanist theologians agree with Moltmann that racism and sexism are sins that consign oppressed persons to spaces and places of inferiority.

He defines sexism as mastery of men over women on the basis of the privileges that they attribute to their manhood. "By analogy to the definition of racism, masculine sexism is to be conceived as masculine pride in one's own sex, favoring the special characteristics of masculinity in culture, the conviction that these characteristics are fundamentally of a biological nature and therefore are determined, combined with the depreciation of women to the 'weaker sex,' the devaluing of presumed 'feminine' attributes, and the exclusion of women from full participation in the life of society."[11] What is especially disheartening is that sexism and its correlate patriarchy is based on the exclusion of women. We noted in ecclesial contexts that although women are present, men speak for them and thereby render them invisible. Moltmann seems to suggest that patriarchy is more insidious than racism in that, it is not as apparent and tends to mask itself in religious garb. I have observed in my teaching that male students, especially White male students, find sexism and the challenge to expose patriarchal ways of being and knowing in the classroom more threatening than the unmasking of racism. I suspect they find the unmasking of patriarchal ways of being and knowing more disruptive of their way of life than a confrontation with racism in the society and church. My sense is that when White students return to their ecclesial or familial contexts after classes, they can choose to ignore racist patterns of exclusion more easily than their own involvement in patriarchal practices. It is also the case that in the classroom it takes more skill and time to identify patriarchal practices than racist patterns of being. Both Moltmann and womanist thinkers note the many ways in which a patriarchal worldview is imbedded in the Scriptures.

Judaeo-Christian culture has been strongly determined by sexism and patriarchy. According to the Tenth Commandment, the wife is included among the property of the (obviously masculine) neighbor, after which the other person—also a man—is not to lust any more than he is after the neighbor's "house, slave, maidservant, ox or ass." This is not exactly flattering for the woman as human and as God's image. Indeed, according to the Priestly source (Gen.1), human beings are created in God's image as "male and female." By this, memory of original equality is immediately obscured again by the yahwist (Gen.2:3): the woman is created second and is the first to fall into sin. As punishment, therefore, the woman is to suffer "pain in childbearing," have "desire for her husband," and "he is to rule over her" (Gen.3:16).[12]

Moltmann, like his womanist counterparts, points out that the Scriptures are suffused with patriarchal assumptions, and make the case that the male is destined to dominate the woman and this is approved by both God and man. It is not surprising then that on the basis of the Scriptures, Christians often make the case that men are superior to women and have a divine right to rule over them. What is of interest here is the way in which the male identity is constructed on the basis of the subjugation of woman. "The characteristics of masculine sexuality are turned into a form of self-justification: complete human being means masculine being. Woman is seen as a being of a lesser rank with lesser capabilities. ... 'She is the wife of the man.'...The domination of man over woman is legitimated by his own sex: man is ordained to leadership, initiative, and mastery. Man's place is in the public world; woman's place is in the home."[13] Womanist thinkers point out that when you add race to this equation in which woman is destined to be ruled by man and to suffer because of her misdeeds, you begin to get a feel for how lonely it must be for the Black woman who in a racist and sexist society does not even measure up to what is being said about womanhood in general. It is as if they are outside the pale of what it means to be the family of God.

Moltmann indicates that the identity of the male oppressor at best is tenuous as it is a negative identity. Man is defined in terms of what he is not. The male oppressor does not only define identity in terms of not being Black but now in terms of not being woman. It is a negative identity. Sexism like racism is also a means of waging psychological warfare on the part of dominating males against dominated females. The male sense of superiority breeds feelings of inferiority in the females and especially in a religious culture and in ecclesial contexts this is often seen as the will of God.

In order to overcome sexism, men must be willing to give up their sexist ways of seeing woman as necessary for the negative definition of self, this need to define self over against woman is construed as narrow-minded, and must be set aside for an identity as human.

The second way to overcome sexism Moltmann sees as similar to the overcoming of racism. What is required is a "redistribution of power" that gives men and women equal access to economic, social, legal, and political opportunities for the realization of what it means to be human. I gather Moltmann would point out that he is addressing oppressors and dealing with what repentance would look like for them. This means then that in a profound sense what he is advocating is for White men to make room for White women, and as we look at the way many institutions are structured in the United States, we could say they have done just that, yet the fundamental problem continues as Black women and other minorities are locked out of the opportunities to which Moltmann alluded. What is required, it seems, is a radical change, change at the root of institutions to create Black sacred space for others who are radically different. In a conversation with oppressors on their terms and being addressed by one who self-defines as an oppressor is not yet to talk about the destruction of institutions that are unwilling or unable to change to make room for the humanity of those who are radically different. In a sense, Moltmann's task was quite easy at the university in the United States in which he made a plea for the liberation of oppressors on their own terms. Because the methodology employed by Moltmann is that "of like appealing to like," in the matter of sexism there is no guarantee that rhetorical space for social democracy is created for those who are different. This is why a fundamental methodological problem of Moltmann was to locate the cross not among those who were crucified with Christ but among those who crucified Christ. The truth is that oppressors, because they lack the desire and the interest in their own liberation, are unable to liberate themselves and others. Womanist thinkers indicate that the liberation of the oppressors is rooted in the freedom of the oppressed who in freeing themselves also set the oppressors free. The truth is that oppressive structures need to be destroyed and it is irrational to believe that oppressors who benefit from these structures would will their destruction. The oppressor is unable to destroy them because he benefits from the harm and the subjugation that these institutions promote in relation to other human beings. The oppressed who have been injured and demeaned and subjugated by these institutions can abolish them and get to the task of building new institutions in which the old arrangements of master and slave, white and black, male and female are no longer determinative of what it means to be human. It is in this sense we may begin to pray, "thy kingdom come on earth as it is in heaven."

Moltmann turns next to what he calls the sin of capitalism from which oppressors need to repent. It is somewhat surprising that although capitalism is the underlying cause for much of the racism meted out to Black people in the New World, Black and womanist theologians have been very silent about a discussion of capitalism and ways it sets brothers and sisters against each other and serve as foundation for patriarchal ways of being. Shayne Lee points out in his important book *America's New Preacher: T.D. Jakes*[14] that the Black church is in danger of losing its soul, as Black pastors see themselves as CEOs in mega-churches running multimillion dollar empires in which there is little care for those on the margins of society. Cone suggests that there is a contradiction of terms as Christian churches are among the most important supporters of capitalism and often fail to demonstrate a commitment to the process of liberation. "For if an economic analysis of our material resources do not reveal our commitment to the process of liberation, how can we claim that the Black church and its theology are concerned about the freedom of oppressed peoples."[15] Both Lee and Cone suggest that the Black church is in danger of functioning like an oppressor in relation to poor people. It is therefore appropriate to join the conversation with Moltmann as he examines another sin of oppressors: capitalism.

Moltmann points out that his main concern is not with the ownership class, as they are content in their privileged state, nor with the proletariat, as many persons including Karl Marx have pointed to their plight, but to focus on the evils of capitalism as it impacts the lives of middle-class persons. While the self-estrangement of the ownership class and the proletariat find its basis in the misuse of power, or more pointedly, on how power functions in the market place, the self-estrangement of the middle class has to do with the deification of vocation, work, success, and the ways in which they point to self-sacrifice. He cites an immigrant who complains about his American father-in-law who resides in Ohio: "Couldn't the old man be satisfied with his $75,000 a year and rest? No! The frontage of the store must be widened to 400 feet. Why? That beats everything, he says. In the evening when his wife and daughter read together, he wants to go to bed. Sundays he looks at the clock every five minutes to see when the day will be over—What a futile life."[16] When life is obsessed with success, it borders on a sense of futility. Moltmann cites Karl Marx:

> Self-denial, the self-denial of life...is its major dogma. The less that you eat and drink, the fewer books you buy, the less that you go to the theatre, the dance, the inn, the less that think, love, theoretize, sing, paint, poetize, etc., the more you save, the greater will become your treasure, which neither moths nor dust can destroy your capital. The less that you exist, the less that you express your life, the more you have, the greater is your externalized life, the more that you hoard your estranged essence.[17]

A basic problem that capitalism engenders is the tendency to confuse being with having. The problem with the resultant estrangement is that often the more we have the less we are. Moltmann cites Martin Luther in the *Large Catechism*:

> To have a God is simply to trust and believe in one with our whole heart. As I have often said, the confidence and faith of the heart alone make both God and idol. If your faith and confidence are right, then likewise your God is the true God. For the two, faith and God, have

inevitable connection. Now, I say, whatever your heart clings to and confides in, that is really your God...Many a one thinks he has God and entire sufficiency if he has money and riches; in them he trusts and proudly and securely boasts that he cares for no one. He surely has a god called mammon...that is, money and riches...upon which he fixes his whole heart. This is a universal idol upon earth.[18]

The key that is being emphasized is that capitalism alienates: it sets up an estrangement between what a person is and the true self.

Capitalism becomes a way of life in which one self-justifies on the basis of work, accomplishment, profit, and progress. This is rather poignant in relation to the practice of pedagogy where students are often identified in terms of their grades. In a capitalistic environment, we are raised with the notion that unless we work hard we will not amount to anything. It is our work that defines us and offers the possibility for us to become someone with worth. "This compulsion always to justify oneself by means of work distorts all trust in human being. Thus children are already put down by saying to them: 'you must work in order to be a success. For you are nothing.'"[19] In this culture we are always told that we have to *make* something of ourselves through work, and often this means academics. And it is what we make of ourselves that defines us. This semester I taught as an adjunct professor at a Black college in Atlanta. During the semester, two of my students at the Black college confided that they were being ejected from their apartments because of their inability to pay rent. They were older students who had to work and attend school at the same time. They acknowledged that their primary emotion was one of shame "that they had not made something of themselves." At the other campus where I also teach, majority of students receive scholarships and parental support, and do not live with this threat of being thrown out of their homes in the middle of the semester. What must we make of this experience of students who were ejected from their homes? I am so close to this negative experience of our students that I am unsure what conclusions to draw as we talk about living with dignity in a capitalist society. What may we say as first words? Did the students who were ejected from their homes in the middle of the semester not count the cost of a seminary education? Should we posit that in a capitalist society, being includes having? Is it naïve to suggest that there is a necessary estrangement between being and having? Does this not place Moltmann's understanding of liberation of oppressors on a collision course with our sense of Christian stewardship? When Black and womanist theologians talk about liberation, they are not only talking about a new estimate of self that ensues from tackling the stubborn realities of racism and sexism, but about tackling poverty and finding a way to ensure that the poor are able to live with dignity. What is instructive for our work is that Moltmann addresses himself not to entities outside our purview, such as corporations and institutions, but to middle-class persons (oppressors), and this category transcends race and gender.

Many Christian churches teach a prosperity gospel aimed at helping parishioners take financial responsibility for their lives. Of course, many of these churches teach that the first responsibility of the Christian is to work hard, and then give a minimum of 10 percent to the church that acts as a custodian for God. The thesis is a very simple and straightforward one that God wants God's people to prosper in all areas of life, but especially financially, and the main test as to whether or not one has an active faith in God, a faith that is pleasing to God, is whether or not one prospers financially. One of the names for God is the one who provides. God is the provider and will not fail God's people if they are faithful in their discipleship to the church. This was the primary reason why the first reaction of the students who were ejected from their home because they were unable to pay their rent was one of shame. The response from the ecclesial community was that their faith in God was suspect, because if they had an active faith God would provide for them "exceedingly abundantly more than they could dream of or think of." The shame also came from their membership in the wider capitalist society in which the myth that guides many persons is that if you work hard enough you can have anything that you desire. To live in the United States of America is to live in the richest country the world has ever seen, this means that there is the opportunity for the church to be rich, and for citizens to be rich. Signs of poverty, it is claimed, are due to laziness and lack of industry.

We may not lose sight of the fact that the two Black students who were put out of their homes for failure to pay rent considered themselves middle class up until their ejection. They had all the trappings of a middle-class lifestyle; credit cards, working as assistant pastors in churches, and membership in a seminary community at one of the prestigious universities in Atlanta. Both students owned cars and were married with children. One of the differences that Moltmann's analysis does not take into account is the difference between the Black and White middle-class status in the United States of America. It is clear in this essay that Moltmann addresses himself principally to White oppressors. But if we take him at his word that attachment to work, vocation, and success, as a way of defining our humanity are signs of what it means to be an oppressor driven by capitalistic aggression, then we must note that being an oppressor is not merely a White trait or problem but a human one. Certainly, when the context is a capitalist society where churches tend to baptize American capitalism and call it Christianity, the matter becomes more complex. What we discover from Moltmann's analysis of capitalism is that the estrangement that one experiences between one's best self and one's actual or existential self is not limited to White people because non-White persons have also internalized this way of being and having in a capitalist environment.

What is Right with the Black Church?

What the students who lost their homes discovered and what they seek to teach us is that there is often a difference between the White and Black middle class in the United States of America. The central difference is that the Black middle class may be just one paycheck away from being put out of their homes because they have not sustained a relationship with an extended family to serve as a safety net in times of crisis. There was a time when the Black church served as that safety net and was a place of refuge for families or individuals in trouble. This was how the Black community in times past made it over the rough waters of slavery, segregation, and economic exploitation. The current problem has to do with the change in the theology of many churches. During slavery and through the long march toward freedom of Black people in the United States, the Black church was shaped by a theology that taught: "God will meet you at your point of need." However one defined one's need, there was a sense that God would meet this need and often the church would stand in for God and minister to the social, economic, and health needs of its parishioners. But with the phenomenon of the mega-churches in the Black community led by Creflo Dollar at the World Changers Ministry, Eddie Long at New Birth Missionary Baptist church, and T.D. Jakes at the Potter's House, the theology has changed from a God who meets God's people at the point of need to a "God of Abundance." The preachers claim that because God is a God of abundance, God wants to do more than meet needs; God is ready "to open the windows of heaven and pour out a blessing on God's people." If you are not the recipient of God's many blessings in terms of houses and cars, the fault is not God's because God is a loving father who is ready to bless God's children. The problem resides with the parishioner and the problem is lack of faith. Many churches teach that the absence of material things—be they cars, houses, and personal security—is at its core the absence of faith in God. One pastor in Atlanta who presides over a mega-church was reported to say: "faith is a Rolls Royce in your parking lot, faith is your possession of a splendid house."

What needs to be said is that in the wider culture in which the Black middle class lives a rather precarious existence in that the distance between being homeless and being middle class is one paycheck away, the prosperity gospel finds a hearing and a following from people who are scared and in need of an overarching myth of prosperity to serve as a cushion from the bad news of economic hardships.

In this context Moltmann's counsel is only partly helpful for the Black church, Black community. It is true one should not deify work, vocation, and success, but if one in spite of middle-class labels is only a paycheck away from poverty, then one may want to begin to question if work, vocation, and success have their source in God. What does it mean to acknowledge God as the source and resource of the fulfilled life? How do we understand God in a capitalist context when we live in the richest country the world has ever seen? Is God the God of abundance? Or is God the one who meets us at the point of need? Does being include having? Is it possible to live with dignity without a measure of materiality? How much is enough?

There are a number of cautionary notes that Moltmann strikes that are helpful as we struggle with what it means to live with dignity in this society and to worship God in this church. There is a danger that in a capitalist culture we may worship the idol of materiality. There is a real danger of placing one's trust in capital rather than in God. There is a danger of seeing capital as source rather than God. He warns of the danger of seeing the future in terms of accumulated riches "The riches that have been saved up cheat a person of a loving and vital life. They are supposed to eliminate anxiety for the future, but instead they increase precisely this anxiety because they depend upon the future and are not able to overcome it."[20] There are not many Black persons who could relate to Moltmann's description of the problems wealth may create in the future. They would rather have those problems than the lack of security and safety to which he alludes. The anxiety that the Black middle class worries about is not related to wealth but the absence of wealth. Emblematic of this anxiety is a number of Black students informing me this semester that they have much catching up to do as they could not afford to buy textbooks at the beginning of the semester. The anxiety is with poverty and the sense of shame of not being able to afford textbooks, heath care, and the ability to have a roof over one's head.

However, another danger from which we may not escape in a capitalistic society is the conjoining of racism, sexism, and capitalism. Black theologians also make this connection when they point out that Black people's fear of White people is not misplaced, as White people control economic power in the United States and have the power in many cases to fire or prevent a promotion, essentially controlling the future of Black people. This is especially poignant when at stake is a Black woman who needs to provide for her children. "Capitalism represents the unlimited, permanent increase of power and therefore the unabated struggle for mastery. The aggressiveness which capitalism encourages in order to build its world must—if we are to pursue this aggression-anxiety thesis—have its source in limitless anxiety, which it presupposes and extends. If this is so then capitalism must be seen as a form—perhaps the ultimate form—of human self-hatred. For the first time in history, the potential for self-destruction and destruction of the earth lies in the hands of alienated human beings. This is what makes the situation so dangerous ..."[21]

If racism, sexism, and capitalism are the cardinal sins middle-class oppressors have to struggle against along with their offspring aggression and anxiety, how may we address the root cause of this problem? How may we avoid the trap of becoming alienated human beings in this ecclesial context and in this society?

Moltmann points out that the answer is not in moral suasion or commitment of the individual or community to turn things around. The problem is ontological; it concerns the nature of what it means to be human in this culture and society. There are three familiar claims that he makes, which serve as a basis for our way forward:

a. Human beings do not merely *have* sins; they are sinners
b. Sin is not a moral error but a *compulsion*; a servitude of the will
c. This faulted mode of being and this compulsion are universal[22]

When evil is understood as the doctrine of sin, it becomes a *doctrine of hope*. This is because sin is not the essence of human nature but a "peculiarity of our history." Sin is not constitutive of our being but an intrusion into a world created by God. The good news as it pertains to human being in this world is that through God sin can be overcome. Sin is not the decisive word about who we are or who we are becoming. Sin points to a good thing having gone bad.

In the midst of life that is affected and shaped by racism, sexism, and capitalism, the church asserts that human beings were created by God and for God. The evils of racism, sexism, and capitalism are not constitutive of what it means to be human. Because human being is being created by and for God, the essence of what it means to be human is love. "Their entire nature is one of passionate love. God is the fullness of their blessedness. The infinite God is the happiness of humankind; and the limitless love of the latter is the joy of God. If this love is withdrawn from God and directed to non-divine beings or things, then unhappiness arises; finite things cannot satisfy infinite love."[23]

Moltmann uses St. Augustine with good effect to remind us that God made humanity for God-self and humanity cannot be fulfilled outside of God. The dilemma that confronts human beings is that God has placed God's infinite love in our hearts and neither finite beings nor things can satisfy the need for God. The turn to racism, sexism, and capitalism are consequences of the turn from God and an attempt to find self in these evils. "From a love that has lost God arises an unquenchable and therefore all-destructive passion—a passion for power and possession. The love that can find no fulfillment is perverted into anxiety. The love that is disappointed in its expectations is perverted into vandalism."[24]

The essence of humanity is the passion for love and this love can only be satisfied in God. Expressions of domination are forms of this love. "For the sake of this love, all crimes are committed and all wars are waged; for its sake people love and hate....The unquenchable hunger of dictators for power and wealth and possession is in truth the love of God."[25]

The resolution of the passion to dominate another and to live alienated lives that are divorced from justice in race and gender relations must find its answer in love anchored in God. "The hunger after power is unquenchable....The will to subjugate is limitless. One must recognize this religious dimension in the phenomena of inhumanity; otherwise one cannot understand the violent passion implanted in such deeds. Racism, sexism and capitalism are religious perversions and show themselves as perverted religions."[26]

Implications for Pedagogy

The implications for pedagogy are quite clear. Our problem is not lovelessness but misplaced love. Pedagogy that is liberative respects the humanity of each person and seeks to exclude racism, sexism, and capitalism from defining what it means to be human in classroom and society, thus pedagogy must become an invitation to love God. The way forward is to begin to realize that God's infinite love is already infused in each person and as persons are treated with respect and permitted to be subjects of their own histories, the possibility of trans-formation breaks through. Each member of the class, as each person in society, is allowed to name God for herself or himself. Each person is subject of his/her action and is encouraged to call God by God's name, perhaps a name derived from the experience of discovering infinite possibilities of love in his/her own history.

This is true for all persons but especially for Black and womanist theologies, the exercise of the freedom to name God and to affirm their subjectivity and intersubjectivity in relation to others and God. The viewing of the self as subject and a stubborn refusal to see self as object opens the door of inclusion for celebration of the love of God "shed abroad in our hearts." This revelation of God's infinite love that takes root in community and in each life provides the courage and empowerment to fight against expressions of racism, sexism, cap-italism, classism, and homophobia. The fight against discrimination and exclusion is another way of fighting against the glorification of institutions and the subjugation of oppressed persons. Moltmann warns oppressors not to speak of masculine aspects of God but to speak of the God who calls into question all our depictions of the divine. As oppressors begin to speak of God they discover that God resides among the lowly. This seems to be the implication of the song of liberation as sung by Mary:

> For the Mighty One has done great things for me, And holy is his name.
> And His mercy is upon generation after generation
> Towards those who fear Him
> He has done mighty deeds with his arm;
> And has scattered those who were proud in the
> thoughts of their heart.
> He has brought down rulers from their thrones,
> And has exalted those who were humble.
> He has filled the hungry with good things;
> And sent away the rich empty-handed (Luke 1:49–53)[27]

But not only are the sins of racism, sexism, capitalism, and classism expressions of misplaced love but distorted forms of trust in God. If one side of what it means to be human is to love and be loved, the other side is to trust and be trusted. "[T]he reciprocal relationship of God and humankind is trust. In what ever one places one's heart and wholly trusts—that is one's 'God.' If the trust is right, then one's God is right....God and faith belong together and condition each other reciprocally."[28] The point being made is that in similar fashion as racism, sexism, and capitalism are distorted forms of love, so also is the lack of trust. "The lack of trust is also always a basic form of trust. Only when I am able to abandon myself *wholly* to something do I know that I am borne up by it and feel free."[29] The challenge is to find someone or something in which one may repose complete trust. The attempt to place trust in finite means be they persons, institutions, or things throws us back on the search for God as God is the only reliable source. "Whoever withdraws her or his trust from the invisible God and places it in visible things falls victim to an unfulfillable compulsion for legitimation. Such a person must constantly reassure himself and be reassured by others that he is somebody, for in himself he's obviously nothing."[30] The fragility of human-centered trust breeds disappointment with self and others and serves as a source for resentment and aggression. "Whoever loses his trust in God must place his fundamental trust in his race, his masculinity or his capital. Because he knows that he is nothing, he directs his entire self-trust onto what he *has*. Ingrained in racism, sexism, and capitalism is a deeply distorted lack of trust and therefore a self-expanding mistrust."[31]

The way forward is a change of relationship to the God who has been abandoned in favor of racism, sexism, and capitalism. But the problem is that oppressors are unable to change this relationship on their own. The truth is that help has to come from God through the cross of Christ. "According to the New Testament, in the messianic mission and in the surrender, suffering and death of Jesus there is revealed the *humanity of God*, who humbles himself, allows himself to be wounded, takes deadly aggression upon himself and becomes a victim, in order to liberate oppressors from the compulsion of degradation."[32] The hope for oppressors has to do with what happened at the cross of Christ, as in the humanity of God that was revealed in the victimization of Christ, the divinity of humanity came to the fore. In Christ the victim who takes on aggression, woundedness, and crucifixion, the divinity of humanity becomes the basis for the emergence of a new community in which the old divisions of master and slave are transcended. Something new happens in this community marked by "discipleship to the cross." It is in the crucified Christ that the oppressor meets the humanity that he has persecuted, oppressed, and stolen.

The oppressor can only discover God in the community of the crucified. "He discovers the God whom he despairingly loves in the victims he has killed out of hatred. The Crucified is the true man and the truth of humanity in an inhuman world. The Crucified is the true God and the truth of God in a godless and idolized world. The humiliated, dishonored, oppressed and sacrificed Christ...corresponds to God in this world of contradictions. Thus, the humanization of the inhuman comes about only through the cross of Christ."[33]

The cross of Christ is located in the community marked by the suffering of God. At the cross the infinite suffering of God finds expression in the victims of power who become the community of the crucified. In this community gathered around the cross of Christ, false loves and false trusts make room for new humanity born out of conformity with the crucified, the one form that transforms distorted humanity.

What follows is "discipleship to the cross of Christ." "The person for whom God has suffered on the cross of Christ, whom he has graced by his judgment, and who has been justified in his existence, dies to his previous life-world. He 'abandons everything' and 'follows after him.'"[34] There is no longer any desire to conform to the ways of the world. It is now the form of Christ made plain in the cross that is the locus of the transformed life. To encounter Christ in this community of suffering means one is willing to take up her cross and follow after Jesus. In following after Jesus the new disciple ceases to follow the ways of racism, sexism, classism, homophobia, and capitalism. These evils die as new humanity is born. "Therefore if anyone is in Christ, he/she is a new creature; the old things passed away; behold, new thing have come" (2Corinthians 5:17). There is an overcoming of the old ways of being and knowing that marked the former existence. A new reality, new being is made possible by conformation to the form of the crucified one.

In this new reality, new humanity, liberation, and freedom are not viewed as mastery over others. Freedom cannot mean lording our views or way of life over others. This view of freedom and liberation keeps intact the old order of master and slave. Education should never be about mastery, but about the awakening of a liberated consciousness, the creation of new spaces for dialogue, and the celebration of community. Freedom must always be a freedom for transformation, a freedom for love and trust that find full expression in community. "I am free when I am acknowledged, accepted and beloved by others. Other persons are free when I acknowledge them and open their lives for them, sharing life with them . . . If freedom is not mastery but rather communion, then unfreedom consists in a hindered, alienated, and distorted communion."[35]

Freedom as mastery makes the oppressor the ideal, because through racism, sexism, classism, and capitalism, he/she seeks to dominate and subjugate. Freedom as participation in community opens the door for love and trust to provide the ties that bind us to God and each other. In this context we will always discover that pedagogy is for transformation.

6

Pedagogy as Celebration

In this book we have looked at the emergence and flowering of Black and womanist theologies and have sought to draw implication for the ways in which they serve as resource for pedagogy. Black theologians claimed that the primary reason for Black theology was the exclusion of the Black religious experience by White religionists in the articulation of White theology. This claim was based on the notion that African and African American culture, including ways of knowing and being, are inherently inferior to White culture and its ways of knowing and being. As Black theologians rejected the exclusionary posture of White religionists they sought to articulate a theology that spoke with specificity to the needs and hopes of the Black community. What surprised these Black male theologians as they sought to craft a Black theology for the entire Black community was that because they worked from the Black male experience, they in fact excluded the religious experiences of Black women. Black theologians were surprised to learn that Black women could not see themselves in their work because they were accustomed in church, society, and now in the academy to speak for women. The practice of Black men representing Black women has for a long time been a way of existing in the home, the church, and the society and therefore was a logical carry over to the academy. Although Black theologians excluded the Black woman as friend, sister, and colleague, Black theologians were careful not to adopt the exclusionary approach of White religionists in relation to White male theologians but included them in the exposition and analysis of Black theology.

Black theology has always exhibited a passion to include the stranger, the critic, the person of a different race and culture. This accommodation of the other is true of most Black theologians who are examined in this book and there has been a firm commitment on their part to engage the stranger and thereby create liberating spaces for dialogue. This embrace of the stranger, I contend, is a carry over from the ethos of Black churches in which diversity is often celebrated as an important value.

When the Black church is at its best, there is always a celebration of the sacrament of hospitality as rhetorical space is created for conversation as persons from diverse backgrounds are included in the ecclesial family. This has been my experience at West Durham Baptist Church in Durham, North Carolina, Decatur African Methodist Episcopal Zion Church in Lithonia, Georgia, and the Covenant Baptist Church in Harlem, New York. There has always been in the Black community a fear that in excluding the stranger one may exclude Christ. In these contexts family and friends are accustomed to defer to and make room for the stranger. The Black church both in its practice and in its new theology finds occasions for the celebration of the stranger.

However, in saying yes to the stranger Black theologians said no to the Black woman who was close at hand. Black women were excluded by Black theologians in the articulation of God-talk that was construed as Black-talk. The truth is that as Black theologians took their cue from the Black church in welcoming and celebrating the other as stranger, they once again followed the lead of the Black church in relegating Black women to the margins. Black women were rendered invisible by Black theologians who sought to speak for and represent Black women before God. In the act of embracing the stranger Black theologians excluded the Black woman as friend and scholar. Throughout this manuscript it is noted in reference to the practice of Black theology the subtle ways in which the act of embrace is often at the same time an act of exclusion especially for persons who are regarded as powerless. Saying yes to a person or community often implies saying no to another.

It is always appropriate in the context of the classroom and in community forums to inquire who is being celebrated: who receives A's and vice versa who is excluded, who receives C's.

Pedagogy for Transformation

The history of Black reality in the United States and in the African Diaspora has been one of exclusion from both the White church and White theology. Black people are not strangers to exclusion, as the very term Blackness became a stumbling block first for the White majority in the United States and then for many Black persons who struggled with the cross of exclusion. To be Black in the New World was to be marginalized, as Blackness was a way of constructing the social reality of enslaved persons who were separated from their land, their languages, their culture, and historical memory. Blackness became a reality in which many Black persons understood a radical divide in themselves between how they understood themselves and how they were being defined.

Existence in relation to the community, land, forest, tribe, and the ancestors was the African way of being in the world, and religion suffused their way of life. For Africans in the New World hell was separation from this way of being and relating. Enslaved persons would sing, "Way down yonder by myself I couldn't hear nobody pray." Hell was exclusion from family, land, forest, ancestors and because of this ontological grounding with the primordial community and the land, suicide was practiced as a way home to Africa, a return to the forest, the community, and the ancestors. John Mbiti reminds us in his important book *African Religions and Philosophy* that Africans take religion with them to the market, the fields, and to the village. Religion suffuses their worldview. With this keen sense of the divine infusing their world there are celebrations in planting seeds, in harvesting crops, birthing and rearing children. Celebrations are a way of life often expressed in festivals, in births, marriages, funerals, and all the time singing and dancing accompany these celebrations.

The Black church ethos remembers Africa. There is much that the Black community celebrates as the Black church functions as its memory and hope. There is a remembering, a recalling of the past that pushes the community to celebration as it looks back at the negative past of slavery that decimated community, and separated Black people from their land and historical memory. One expression of the loss of community in the Americas is the capitalist emphasis on the individual, and a sense that one has to be a rugged individual to survive in the United States. This focus on the individual has not been helpful for the practice of family and communal ways of being in this society. The teaching of the wider society, that if one works very hard and applies oneself, one can become a millionaire is a part of the capitalist myth that teaches Black people to place their trust and faith in things as the community reaches for security rather than to learn to trust God and communal values. This individualistic ethic is neither African nor biblical, it places confidence not in God as center of value or in relation with others in community, but in things that in the long run prove to be unreliable. This expression of the capitalist myth that hard work by industrious individuals is the key to meaning making and the good life circumvents the gospel message that God is our source of life and joy. The capitalistic individualistic ethic offers work and financial security as a way of planning the future. But the gospel informs us that it is not the God of materiality that secures the future but the creator God who has "the whole world in God's hand." The Black church in its zeal to exit traditions of poverty and economic hardships must be careful lest it worships at the shrine of the God of materiality. What is at stake is the saving of the soul of America and the celebration of ecclesial communities of memory and hope.

There is another problem with the individualistic ethic as it finds expression in the Black church. The problem has to do with the Christianization of the notion of the rugged individual that as I mentioned is neither African ("We are therefore I am") nor Biblical ("seek ye first the realm of God"), which in many churches is subsumed in the expression "We must come to Jesus one by one." Many Black churches teach that we must come to God singly or God will not accept us. This Christianization of the rugged individual deemphasizes community as it sets brother against brother and sister against sister and locks us into a competition to see who will make it first to the kingdom of materiality and who will receive A's and who will receive C's.

It seems to me that the time has come for the Black church and academy to move from an individualistic ethic to a communal one if the community is to teach and declare the good news of the redeemed individual and not continue to perpetuate the myth of the rugged individual. Both church and academy must begin to teach that the individual is redeemed not as the self becomes referential of the good life but as it is restored to the community.[1] I have often asked my students what it would look like to pray that God would save the university as community rather than to pray for individual salvation. Why not pray that a city such as Atlanta would be saved? Must God save us one by one?

We also celebrate the survival of the Black family and the passion for wholeness in the community. In spite of its travails and tragedies the Black family gave us our "sheroes" and heroes, Fannie Lou Hamer, Harriet Tubman, Rosa Parks, David Walker, Denmark Vesey, Martin Luther King, Jr., and Ella Baker, Jo Ann Robinsom among others. We celebrate the institution of family and the central role the Black family has in conserving and passing on the values of Black power, pride, and love for self and others.

There is much to celebrate in the context of the Black community. We celebrate Black survival in Christian America, which has sought in many ways to destroy Black existence because of its hatred and disease with Blackness as a symbol of what they perceive to be wrong with Black people. Christian America's struggle with Blackness exposed the sin of racism in which the Black family had to struggle in slavery with the threat of genocide. It is strange yet true that Christian America through its theology of White superiority and Black inferiority sought to render Black people inhuman. This is certainly one reason why it is something of an anomaly to speak of Black existence as Christian. The embrace of Christianity by Black people in spite of its threat to Black community points to the courage of the cross. The courage at the cross is Black people allowing the suffering of the cross to shape their identity.

Christian churches have throughout the years contrived many arguments from the Bible to justify their claims pertaining to subhuman status of Black people. In the previous chapter Jurgen Moltmann helped us understand what it means to construe the theological task from the perspective of the oppressor class. According to Moltmann the oppressor self-justifies his alienated existence on the basis of love for self and a commitment to exercise power over others. Moltmann points out that only God is able to love the oppressor with a consuming love that burns away self-hatred. God's love for the oppressor is expressed as God's judgment of evil and anxiety. We have learned from Martin Luther King , Jr., that we dare not make peace with evil as it will destroy us. The temptation is to coexist with evil; the challenge is to participate with God in overcoming the temptation to do nothing about structures of evil.

Black theology must celebrate the "hush arbors" where the slave preachers reinterpret the gospel for enslaved persons as they sought to make sense of the teaching of the Christian church. This was the incipient stage of the Black church. But as we celebrate the survival and presence of the Black church we recall the counsel of womanist theologians that although the Black church has been "our bridge over troubled waters" it has often mimicked the ways of the wider culture and the White church. Although Black women comprise the majority population of most Black churches, their leadership in these churches is not commensurate with their numbers. Further, in most Black churches women are excluded from ministerial leadership. In many of these churches women are forbidden to serve the sacraments or to preach. Many of these Black denominations continue to refuse to ordain women to the Christian ministry. The church of God in Christ excludes women from ordination as part of its official policy although there are a few of these churches that contravene this policy. Even in cases where women are ordained they still have difficulty finding employment as pastors. Sometimes they will be appointed as assistant pastors or as associates in Christian education.

The hospitality that is accorded the stranger is not given to the Black woman in the Black church. Black womanist theologians identify the problem as sexism, which points to a patriarchal way of viewing the world. This worldview allows men to speak for women and to posit the male as ontologically superior to women. In many Christian churches the worldview of male superiority is predicated on the notion of the maleness of God. It is humbling to acknowledge that Christian teaching is largely responsible for the notion that women are essentially inferior to men as men reflect the fullness of the image of God in ways that are unavailable to women.

There is also still extant in the preaching and teaching traditions of many Black churches concerning the theological claims that women are ordained by God to be obedient and subject to their husbands. In many ecclesial settings women are reminded that Eve was the first to sin and a part of what this means is that women are emotionally inferior to men. This theological orientation claims that women cannot be trusted to be dispassionate or to make decisions that entail reflective analysis. In many religious contexts the unspoken assumption is that men must represent women because the divine image is male, therefore women are to understand their identity in light of the maleness of God. Perhaps this was an unarticulated reason for the silencing of the voices of Black women by Black theology and Black church practice.

The way forward in church as in society is for Black women to find their own voice and begin to carve out their own theology and witness to the patriarchal bias in scriptures that allows us to talk about God and humanity from a male point of reference.

The observant student may ask in the light of this catalog of ways of putting women down in the church and in the wider culture, what if anything is there to celebrate in this church and in this culture? Further, the insistence of womanist thinkers in the church and also in the light of a new consciousness that is pervasive of Black theological discourse, we are led to inquire in what sense has the *novum* broken into history. How may we in church and in classroom witness to the new thing that God is doing in our midst? In what ways may we celebrate the leadership of our women in the academy and in the church in spite of the negative history of oppression undergirded by church teaching and popular culture?

Pedagogy and the Situation of Faith

The situation of faith from which women and men teach and learn in mutuality is a sign and signal of pressure against old ways of thinking and being in church and world. The attempt to relate the grace of God articulated in the gospels to the situation of oppression and suffering in which the people of God seek to make sense signals that not only is a revolution of sorts taking place through the new theologies being produced by the daughters and sons of former slaves, but at the universities and colleges the new is also breaking in as Black women and Black men are beginning to help create Black sacred spaces for the emancipation and liberation of the community. Students are no longer expected like parrots to repeat the wisdom of their teachers but are encouraged to think critically, that is, to think their own thoughts and discover that they can change history and take responsibility for the creation of a new language that represents a new reality. Both at the university and at the church we must insist on new ways of thinking and relating. The old order of experts and learners must give way to the in breaking of a community of scholars in which all members are valued and encouraged through their stories to participate in the production of new knowledge. The bottom line has to do with knowledge of self-world and a commitment to transform this world. This is especially important when we are dealing with the Black church as a "Black sacred cosmos" where tradition tends to hold sway. It is precisely at this point that we are grateful to womanist thinkers to point out and point up the negative uses of tradition, the ways in which tradition may prevent growth and stand in the way of emancipation of those who are most vulnerable in our community. It is at this point that tradition must be placed in conversation with the need of the community for wholeness and liberation. The uncritical use of tradition as it is with the uncritical use of scripture can be the greatest hindrance for the transformation of male/female relations in the academy and in the wider culture at large. Pedagogy as critical thinking must be daring. It must be willing to press against limits as new ways of thinking are coupled with new ways of acting.

One of the realities that weigh heavily on my mind is students in college investing time and energy in receiving an education but having to work forty hours per week. It is very difficult for these students to give of their best when they have not learned how to be fully present as work always comes between them and their education. It is also unfortunate that in most cases the work performed is unrelated to their studies. Many schools have the resources to alter this world for the students and make it possible for the student to be fully present and give full time to her studies. A similar situation portends in the ecclesial community where many women are being prepared at the university and seminary for jobs in the church and in the wider culture, and although they are superb students on graduation often because of their gender, they are denied employment. Critical thinking in relation to these two problems means finding new ways of thinking and acting to resolve these contradictions. Liberation and emancipation must mean new ways of acting and thinking in our world that provide a basis for human flourishing. The new that womanist and Black theologians help to forge in relation to racism, sexism, classism, capitalism, and homophobia was the calling into question of a perverted and distorted view of humanity that had as its frame of reference the justification of the self in relation to things and the uses of power. The bottom line was the glorification of the self at the price of the subjugation of others. What womanist and Black theologies achieved as modes of critical thinking was to expose the wretchedness of the human situation that was often covered up and hidden by an appeal to scripture, tradition, and a false anthropology. In the context of ecclesial communities theology became ideology as God-talk became a way to justify the distorted and perverted ways of relating. Theology was used to keep intact relationships in which persons were subjugated and encouraged to continue in contexts in which they were humiliated and diminished.

Another way to get at what I am seeking to portray is that the classroom often serves as a context in which class differences among students get reified, and students who accept the status of being lower class as they may be unable to navigate their way through the maze of intellectual jargon being bandied around become silent and mute. Often the real problem is hidden—the oppressive structure of the class and the way in which language and intellectual discourse serves as a weapon to keep students in their place—and blamed on the inability of the student to think critically. Critical thinking would include new ways of relating and of using language as a tool of liberation. The danger I am trying to identify here is that most times the real situation of oppression is hidden and in ecclesial contexts is covered with faith talk—notions of "we are all Americans" or "we are family"—while there is no celebration of opportunities for the gifts of all to be affirmed. For example, I have discovered in the context of the classroom that students are excellent teachers and I begin to see part of my responsibility as a member of the class to accommodate student participation at the level of instruction. This is especially important in the teaching of seminars with graduate students who are in preparation for vocations as teachers. The challenge is how to translate an idea even when it is a liberating idea into praxis. In the classroom we celebrate the idea but we are mindful of the ways in which an idea may hide the true reality of inequality, exclusion, and suffering that are realities in every classroom. "The word must become flesh." The idea must take on praxiological intent. The important pedagogical insight we learn from Black and womanist theologians in relation to critical thinking is that it is inadequate for critical thinking to concern itself only with the meaning of an idea; critical thinking must go the next step, and as womanist theologian Katie Cannon points out, a liberating idea must also be about unmasking and uncovering reality. The key is that the teacher who aims at emancipatory pedagogy must do more than explain an idea, but must show how this idea becomes incarnate in reality and thereby transforms reality.

I would like to look briefly at a short essay by womanist theologian Katie Geneva Cannon, "Transformative Grace," in which she illustrates the importance of an idea becoming incarnate in the existential situation if the outcome anticipated is transformation of social reality. Cannon points out that for a long time as a churchwoman she knew that the word grace was one of the important terms in her church's vocabulary but the way it was defined was not in relation to the real life situation of oppressed people in her community. There was a disconnect between the expression of this term grace and the *sitz im leben* (situation in life) in which she and her people struggled for meaning:

> As black Presbyterians, grace was the basic motif of our lives. I have long known that grace is an unmerited gift from God. However, not until recently did I understand grace as sacred, life transforming power for those of us whose identities are shaped by multiple forces at odds with the dominant culture, primarily those of race, sex, and class.

God's freely given gift of grace enables us to resist the forces of death and degradation arrayed against us and to affirm our dignity as beloved persons created in the image of God.[2]

Cannon points out the challenges of being Black and Presbyterian, the problem of being a Black minority in a White denomination is that one lives with the challenges of invisibility, exclusion, racism, and having to justify one's presence. In this context marked by invisibility, loss of voice, and social death, there is a danger for words to hide real situations of suffering and the added problem of focusing on an explanation of meanings hidden in words rather than allow words and ideas to interrogate situations of wretchedness. There is always an easy temptation for the Black intellectual to see the task of critical thinking as an explication of the meaning of terms and words rather than the joining of theory and practice in the life situation as oppressed persons press for liberation. Cannon explains:

> Mainstream American Presbyterianism has often promoted abstract, disembodied notions of grace that do nothing to address the structures of domination against which African American Presbyterians struggle. African American Presbyterians like Garnet, Blyden, and Robinson rejected stereotypical rhetoric about African peoples, both on the continent and throughout the Diaspora, and articulated understandings of grace that responded to the existential realities of Black people.[3]

While pedagogy celebrates the liberating possibilities of an idea, especially an idea such as grace that seeks to communicate to people who are marginalized that there is an horizon of hope as one is accepted in spite of the odds marshaled against one's life, even a powerful idea like grace can be alienating if we refuse to allow the idea, the "word to become enfleshed." We constantly struggle with divided realities in the classroom, the distance between the way things appear to be and what they really are. Another way to speak of this split in reality is to talk about "isness" and "oughtness." I was quite embarrassed recently when one of my bright Black female students informed me that she was surprised to learn that I was unaware that she was homeless last semester. She had problems accessing a financial package that was promised her by the school. How could I have missed this as her academic advisor, especially since I teach classes in liberation pedagogy? It is at this point that Katie Cannon points out that grace has to be more than a word, liberation has to be more than a word, because words may only be liberating if they are "enfleshed," that is, if they are related to the existential reality students and others struggle for meaning. I asked myself, how could I as teacher, facilitator, be accountable to others for the well-being of my students in a class in which liberation is not just an idea in a book but an organizing principle for pedagogy, and not become aware that a student lives on the boundary of life and death where her dignity is circumscribed and we continue to talk about liberation without any relevance to her life situation?

This is the problem with much classroom practice today. There is a split between the role of ideas and the existential situation that confronts members of the class. Members of the class are often struggling with issues of meaninglessness, death, and the loss of dignity, and there is no space for dialogue about the meaning of their lives.

It is not that an ethic of care is not one of the aims of classroom pedagogy. The problem is that the method of education employed does not seek to discuss ideas in the existential context of relationships. I am aware that one of the limitations many teachers have to live with is that the models we use in the classroom are often based on the teaching styles of our more favorite teachers. In most of my undergraduate and graduate education the teacher would appear in class, read a lecture, and if there was time entertain questions about what he said, and then leave. The lecture was essentially a word from above that had nothing to do with who we are as members of the class and the life and death issues with which we were struggling. There was no space in the classroom for us—teacher and students—to be human together. There was this profound split between our existential reality and the aims and objectives the teacher had for the class. It is precisely at this point that it is appropriate to ask: what is education for? Is it to prepare students to get jobs? Is it a forum for the display of the teachers' knowledge and agenda? Usually in these classes nothing new happens and part of the reason nothing happens is that pedagogy is disconnected with the project to be human. In this context education is aimed at keeping things the way they are. There are no spaces created for new meanings to emerge. Pedagogy is not in the service of the vocation to be human. No one asks concerning the interest of students. Because of this in the classroom, we use words that are not related to the life situation of members of the class. No one bothers to ask: What is education for? The failure to ask concerning the meaning of education forecloses the future and makes pedagogy irrelevant. We experience reality as history and for many of us who live on the boundary between life and death, poverty and the struggle for dignity, it is often the negative uses of history that shrouds our existence.

The problem becomes even more complicated when we turn to ecclesial contexts and experience the disconnect between the meaning of faith as this is enshrined in words and rituals and the meaning of the real life situation. Katie Cannon illuminates the problem for us as she reminds us that the main problem in classroom as in ecclesial contexts is that we do not really want to know the *truth* about the real life situation. The search for truth would force us to relook at pedagogical strategies and test their adequacy for liberation and transformation. If I were interested in the truth about the real world in which my student lives, I would be confronted with the *uncomfortable truth* about her situation. Then I would have to face the question concerning the meaning of education. Is education for transformation? How may we as members of the class participate in repairing and restoring her dignity?

Cannon highlights the tension between the meaning of faith (idea) and the meaning of the real situation:

> Each and every morning I stood tall, crossed my heart, and pledged allegiance to the flag of the United States of America. I recited the Lord's Prayer, quoted the Beatitudes, and answered questions from the Missouri Synod Lutheran catechism. Yet at the same time I lived in a world that demanded and commanded that I go to the back of the bus even though I paid the same fare. Before the age of five, the unbending social codes of conduct between blacks and whites required that I go through back doors and drink out of "colored" water fountains. This racial etiquette was traumatic, and it was violent. So complete was the circle of segregationist laws, the rigidly enforced codes of white supremacy, that it was against the law for me to play in tax-supported public schools.[4]

There was no attempt to join the truth enshrined in the Lord's Prayer, ("thy kingdom come on earth as it is in heaven") with the truth of her real life situation; having to enter White people's homes though the back door, sitting in the back of the bus, and unable as a five year old to play in the school park because of the color of her skin. The student whose eyes are opened can begin to see that pedagogy that does not allow the discussion of ideas to raise questions about the ordering of society is political ideology. It has an agenda, that of keeping things the way they are. "White supremacist ideology is based first and foremost on the degradation of black bodies in order to control them. One of the best ways to instill fear in people is to terrorize them. Yet this fear is best sustained by convincing them that their bodies are ugly, their intellect is inherently underdeveloped, their culture less civilized and their future warrants less concern than that of other peoples."[5]

Cannon brings us back to the basic question of this chapter: How may the idea (doctrine) become inseparable from the practical and ethical situation? We are counseled that the idea has to be more than an explanation of its place in the history of ideas. It has to do more than facilitate discussion for the sake of discussion. She asks us to ponder what grace means when one is set aside as an ugly body, regarded as a person with an underdeveloped intellect, seen as belonging to a culture that is uncivilized, and characterized as one whose future is not worth talking about. In this context grace means more than reciting the Lord's Prayer or repeating the creed on Sunday morning. Grace must mean confronting the sinfulness of the existential situation in which one is homeless or defined as an ugly body. Confronting the situation has to mean more than interpreting the existential reality as sinful. One of the practices teachers and students often engage in the classroom is a comparative analysis of placing the existential real life situation in conversation with a similar situation in another historical period or context and then draw conclusions and then go on to another task. The problem with this methodology is that it leaves the situation unchanged. This methodology serves the interests of the status quo. The truth then is that many teachers because of the methodology they employ are servants of the status quo, whether acknowledged or not, their pedagogy represents a political ideology that keeps the social arrangement of society the way it is.

Theory and Practice in the Service of Pedagogy

What are required are new ways of thinking and new ways of acting. Theory and practice must be conjoined. "First and foremost, grace is a divine gift of redeeming love that empowers African Americans to confront shocking, absurd, death-dealing disjunctions in life, so that when we look at our outer struggles and inner strength we see interpretive possibilities for creative change. Second, grace is the indwelling of God's spirit that enables Christians of African descent to live conscious lives of thanksgiving, by deepening our knowledge of forgiveness given in Christ...."[6] The unity of knowing and doing, the conjoining of the idea with the practical and the ethical means that Black persons along with others may exult in the joy of knowing that the oppressive situation does not have the final or decisive word about their future. The good news is that the old oppressive order is on its way out and the new realm of God is breaking in as African Americans participate in the practice of liberation. Grace is embodied in the practice of liberation as the oppressed name the conflicts in the existential situation and work for a new humanity. Grace is identifying with those who are homeless, naked, hungry, those with ugly bodies and discovering among them the form of the crucified Christ. Grace becomes an occasion for thanksgiving as oppressed persons discover that the social arrangements in society are created by those who have an interest in keeping things the way they are.

Because the structures of oppression are made and kept in place by oppressors the oppressed are thankful that these structures can be changed because they do not have ontological status. These structures do not have a divine origin, they are temporal and therefore can be changed. The longing for change is a characteristic of the yearning for something new to happen in history. The children of Israel in Pharaoh's Egypt longed for change from the oppressive conditions, which defined their lives for many years. Exodus meant setting out with Yahweh on a journey and leaving behind social and political oppression; this is what faith must mean as it becomes incarnate in the real life situation. Faith means leaving Egypt.

The implications for pedagogy is that as a community of scholars we must be clear that our project is the overthrow of conditions and structures that limit our freedom to be human. The test of a liberative pedagogy is that it must have as its goal the changing of the context in which we live out our vocation to be human. Our vocation as human beings is not to flee the world and retreat in safe havens but to name the world and transform it. This is the pedagogical import of Katie Cannon's narration and sharing of her story of grace and oppression. She named evil: racism, sexism, and classism and then as grace became incarnate in the community of oppressed persons the struggle for liberation and transformation ensued.

In the context of the classroom we must ask, what does it mean to name evil, to call racism, homophobia, and sexism by name? What are the practices that need to be changed? Quite recently three female members of my class in systematic theology formed a panel on womanist theology and were responsible for the teaching and learning that happened that day. They indicated that they were tired of having to explain themselves all the time to a community that was predominantly White. They observed that there was an unspoken expectation on the part of their White peers that they would explain how women who are Black and poor happened to be at this school. These women indicated that they caught themselves in the habit of introducing themselves as Black and female, and even when they did not verbally introduce themselves in this way, they acted out the reality. They challenged the White students in the class to practice introducing themselves for the next two weeks as White and male or as White and female. White students were asked to try this way of identifying self when they called the doctor's office, the admission's office, or when they contacted their local police. The class discussion that ensued observed that this was especially poignant in the local news when the media reports a crime. The students noted that when a crime is perpetrated by a White person, his/her race would not be acknowledged, the newscaster would say a man or a woman. But in the case of a minority person the race would always be identified. Students asked if this was one way in which the wider culture called attention to an assumed humanity that belongs to White people and on the other hand calls into question the humanity of others. Is it because of the perception by the dominant culture that a White person's humanity is intact that White people do not have to explain their presence? The Black women said they were tired of having to justify their presence all the time. In a profound sense the students were voicing an old problem in the Black community that of always seeing self through the eyes of others. W.E.B. DuBois states the problem:

> It is a peculiar sensation, this double-consciousness, this sense of always looking at one's self through the eyes of others, of measuring one's soul by the tape of the world that looks on in amused contempt and pity. One ever feels this twoness—an American, A Negro; two souls, two thoughts, two unreconciled strivings; two warring ideals in one dark body, whose dogged strength alone keeps it from being torn asunder.[7]

The class agreed that the grace to which Cannon alludes should be practiced in our class as we create spaces for dialogue in which we name evil and demeaning practices that forces members of the class to always have to explain themselves as if their humanity is in doubt. Students wanted to cultivate the practice of talking about self without reference to an alienating other. This would mean discovering new ways to talk about the Black female body that does not need considerations of race or gender as frame of reference but affirms the body as site of grace. "Grace is the indwelling of God's spirit that enables Christians of African descent to live conscious lives of thanksgiving, by deepening our knowledge of forgiveness given in Christ, so that even in situations of oppression we celebrate the status of imago Dei."[8] Grace means that we are set free to accept ourselves without apologizing for our presence or having a need to explain our presence in reference to race, gender, class because God accepts us as we are. When the classroom and ecclesial context become Black sacred space, all bodies are welcomed. This I believe has been one of the special gifts of Black churches over the years to America that of providing sacred space where all persons are invited and welcomed to accept themselves as they learn that God who created them accepts them. It is this knowledge of being accepted and affirmed by the divine "in the midst of us" that provides a basis for thanksgiving in spite of the oppressive situation in which one seeks to make sense of his/her existence. In the Black ecclesial context weary travelers find rest and many who have been alienated from themselves find a healing presence.

The class felt that this practice of affirming one's identity and humanity through the grace of God would be one step in the direction of overthrowing structures that demean and diminish members of the community. This called for a celebration of pedagogy.

The female students who dared to share their suffering reminded the class of "courage at the cross" exemplified by the women who went with Jesus all the way to the cross. "But there were standing by the cross of Jesus His mother, and His mother's sister, Mary the wife of Clopas, and Mary Magdalene" (John 19:25). These women who were with Jesus during his ministry followed him all the way in spite of Good Friday and the tragedy of crucifixion remained faithful to the end. Most of the disciples ran from the sight of the cross as the form of the crucified, the grotesque, the tragedy of crucifixion proved too much for them. It is this courage of the women at the cross that calls us to recognize our own suffering in the eyes of brothers and sisters and together carry the cross of Christ. As we struggle with the cross of Christ we identify our silence in contexts that are stultifying and our invisibility in settings that seek to make us doubt our identity as the family of God.

But "the break through of grace" is found through the courage that the cross mediates. In spite of Good Friday the women who made it all the way to the cross continued to love Jesus and to care for his body. Black people have been able to identify with these women and sing in many churches:

> Were you there when they crucified my Lord?
> Were you there when they crucified my Lord?

Oh! Sometimes it causes me to tremble, tremble, tremble;
Were you there when they crucified my Lord?
Were you there when they nailed him to the tree?
Were you there when they pierced him in the side?
Were you there when He bowed his head and died?

In the church in which I was raised we sang this song almost every Sunday and most of us would cry as we identified completely with the suffering of Jesus. The answer is we were there, we were eyewitness, we shared in the courage at the cross as we made the cross of Christ our own.

I had a teacher in high school who constantly said she was "allergic to suffering." I believe that if you are able to journey to the first century through your sanctified imagination and identify with Jesus and like the women at the cross spend time with Jesus in his dying, then as this teacher who attended the local Baptist church and testified most Sundays through songs that she was there when Christ was crucified, then an allergic reaction to suffering would be unavoidable. What my teacher meant was that she could not see children wither and become ill because of poverty and diseases and fail to act to change the situation. Often when students doubted that they could make it through the semester because of low self-esteem and a home that was unresponsive to their needs, Ms. Francis was not only teacher but became social worker and motivator. She became whatever we needed her to become in order to help us make it through the long summers of neglect and need. She gave us voice and often helped in repairing a self-image that was badly compromised by difficult social and economic hardships. Sometimes she was our voice as she assumed the role of advocate and interpreter on our behalf. But all the time, especially in her class and in her presence, as students we found the courage to speak and to be ourselves. In her class we were free to risk, to make mistakes, to laugh, to cry, to be ourselves. She gave us permission to be our beautiful complex selves. Her role as teacher was much more than sharing information and keeping discipline. Teaching was sharing herself, her dreams, her fears and hopes with us, and providing a creative context in which we could join her in the vocation to be human.

I often wonder what sustains teachers like Ms. Francis. What prevents them from being overwhelmed with the many challenges the classroom and life brings their way. This is a form of the question we ask the women who followed Jesus not only during his earthly ministry but went all the way to the cross in spite of Good Friday and the crucifixion. What is it that sustains faithful teachers who are willing to go all the way in spite of Good Friday? I believe Katie Cannon hinted in the direction of the secret power that sustained Ms. Francis and the women at the cross. It is grace as the indwelling of the Holy Spirit who empowers and enables us to overcome "the vicious circles of death."

The miracle was that in spite of inadequate resources, a school building that would leak when it rained, low pay,—I now understand there were times when teachers were not paid—lack of appreciation by parents and students, teachers like Ms. Francis never lost faith in their project of making us whole human beings who were committed to leave the world a little better than we found it. These teachers were able against the odds to enable us students to claim our vocation to "survive with dignity" in the midst of strange circumstances because they were empowered and enabled by spirit power. "But you will receive power when the Holy Spirit has come upon you" (Acts.1:8–9). The "secret power" for those who teach and for those who learn is that the Holy Spirit will guide and make us aware of the exigencies, which is sure to confront us on this journey called life. The secret power gives us the courage at the cross to be faithful and to face the truth of the situation. Together we learn that through the agency of Spirit power we may embrace each other with courage at the cross.

Notes

Introduction

1. James Cone, *Risks of Faith*, Boston, MS: Beacon Press, 1999.
2. bell hooks, *Teaching to Transgress*, New York and London: Routledge, 1994.
3. J. Deotis Roberts, "Liberating Theological Education: Can Our Seminaries Be Saved?" *Christian Century*, 100, No. 4, February 2–9, 1983: 98, 113–116.
4. Ibid., 115.
5. Ibid., 116.
6. Ibid.
7. Cecil Wayne Cone, *The Identity Crisis in Black Theology*, Nashville, TN: AMEC Sunday School Union, 1975.
8. James H. Cone, *Martin and Malcolm and America: A Dream or a Nightmare*, Maryknoll, NY: Orbis Books, 1991.
9. Martin Luther King, Jr., "The Ethical Demands for Integration," in *A Testament of Hope: The Essential Writings of Martin Luther King, Jr.*, ed. James M. Washington, San Francisco: Harper & Row, 1986, 122.
10. Ibid., 118–119.
11. Cone, *Martin and Malcolm and America*, 278.
12. James Cone "The Gospel and the Liberation of the Poor," *Christian Century*, February 1, 1981: 162–166.
13. See *New American Standard Bible*.
14. James H. Cone, "Introduction," in *Black Theology: A Documentary History, 1966–1979*, 363.
15. Ibid., 363, 365.
16. Cone, "The Gospel and the Liberation of the Poor," 165.
17. Jacquelyn Grant "Black Theology and the Black Woman," in *Black Theology: A Documentary History, 1966–1979*, ed. Cone and Wilmore, 420.
18. Ibid.
19. Ibid., 421.
20. Ibid., 421, 422.
21. Jacquelyn Grant, *White Women's Christ and Black Women's Jesus*, Atlanta: Scholars Press, 1989, 63–64.

1   Pedagogy and Black Community

1. Preston N. Williams, "The Ethics of Black Power," in *Quest for a Black Theology*, ed. James J. Gardiner and J. Deotis Roberts, Sr., Philadelphia, PA: Pilgrim Press, 1971, 85.
2. See "Black Power" Statement, National Committee of Negro Churchmen, *The New York Times*, July 31, 1966.
3. King, "The Ethical Demands of Integration," in *Testament of Hope*, 122.
4. Ibid., 118–119.
5. Ibid., 119.
6. For an explication of this position see James Cone's *Martin, Malcolm and America*.
7. King, "Facing the Challenge of a New Age," in *Testament of Hope*, 140.
8. King, "Remaining Awake through a Great Revolution," in *Testament of Hope*, 269.
9. King, "Where Do We Go From Here," in *Testament of Hope*, 246.
10. Martin Luther King, Jr., *Strength to Love*, Cleveland, Ohio: Collins Publishers, 1963, 70.
11. King, "I See the Promised Land," in *Testament of Hope*, 283.
12. Ibid.
13. Martin Luther King, Jr., *The Trumpet of Conscience*, New York: Harper & Row, 1967, 14.
14. For a full exposition of this line of reasoning, see Anthony B. Pinn, *Terror and Triumph: The Nature of Black Religion*, Minneapolis, MN: Fortress, 2003.
15. Martin Luther King, Jr., *Stride Toward Freedom*, San Francisco: Harper & Row Publishers, 1958. 195.
16. See "Remaining Awake through a Great Revolution," in *Testament of Hope*, 270.
17. See "I See The Promised Land," in *Testament of Hope*, 283.
18. Lerone Bennett, Jr., *Before the Mayflower*, Baltimore, MD: Penguin Books, 1973, 30–31.
19. James H. Cone, *Black Theology and Black Power*, New York: Seabury Press, 1969, 96.
20. J. Deotis Roberts, *Liberation and Reconciliation*, Louisville, Kentucky: Westminster, John Knox Press, 2005, 76.
21. See James H. Cone "The Easy Conscience of America's Churches on Race," in *Spirituality Justice*, ed. Bill Thompson, reprint, January–February 2003. Chicago, IL: CTA, 3.
22. Ibid.
23. Ibid., 2.
24. Ibid., 3.
25. Ibid.
26. Ibid., 4.
27. Ibid., 5.
28. Ibid., 6.

29. See Cornel West, "Black Theology and Human Identity," in *Black Faith and Public Talk*, ed. Dwight N. Hopkins, Waco, TX: Baylor University Press, 2007, 15–16.
30. Cone, *Black Theology and Black Power*, 18.

2 What Can a Black Woman Teach Me?

1. Gayraud S. Wilmore and James H. Cone, *Black Theology: A Documentary History, 1966–1979*, Maryknoll, NY: Orbis Books, 1979, 7.
2. Stacy Floyd-Thomas, "Redemptive Difference: What Can a Black Woman Teach Me," in *Religious Studies News*, October 2007, 22, No. 4: iii.
3. Ibid.
4. Kelly Delaine Brown-Douglas, "Womanist Theology: What is its Relationship to Black Theology," in *Black Theology: A Documentary History, Vol. 2 1980–1992*, ed. Cone and Wilmore, 290.
5. Ibid., 291.
6. Ibid.
7. Ibid.
8. Ibid., 291, 292.
9. See Karl Barth, *Church Dogmatics*, vol. 4, part 1, Edinburgh: T & T Clark, 1961, 703.
    I am grateful to George Hunsinger for a lengthy discussion in which we agreed that Barth in an attempt to regard theology as transcendent to culture neglected culture hence his claim there is no African Christianity.
10. "Womanist Theology: What is its Relationship to Black Theology," 292.
11. Ibid., 292.
12. Ibid., 293.
13. See Patricia Hill Collins, "Learning from the Outsider Within," in *Beyond Methodology*, eds. Mary Margaret Fonow and Judith A. Cook. Bloomington, IN: Indiana University Press, 1991, 35–59.
14. Ibid., 35.
15. See *Black Theology: A Documentary History, 1966–1979*, 368–376.
16. Ibid., 370.
17. Ibid.
18. See "Womanist Theology: What is its Relationship to Black Theology," 294.
19. Ibid., 294, 295.
20. Ibid., 295.
21. Ibid.
22. Ibid.
23. See *Black Theology and Black Power*, 151, 152.
24. Linda E. Thomas, "Womanist Theology, Epistemology, and a New Anthropological Paradigm," in *Living Stones in the Household of God*, Minneapolis, MN: Fortress Press, 2004, 37–48.
25. Ibid., 38.

26. Linda E. Thomas, "Womanist Theology, Epistemology, and a New Anthropological Paradigm," in *Living Stones in the Household of God*, Minneapolis, MN: Fortress Press, 2004, 39.
27. Ibid.
28. Ibid.
29. Ibid., 41.
30. Ibid., 42.
31. James H. Cone and Gayraud S. Wilmore, eds., *Black Theology: A Documentary History, Vol. 2, 1980–1992*, Maryknoll, NY: Orbis Books, 1993, 345–351.
32. Ibid., 346.
33. Ibid.
34. Ibid.
35. Ibid., 347.
36. Ibid., 349.
37. Ibid., 350.

3   Pedagogy and Ontological Sameness

1. Kimberly Eison Simmons, "A Passion for Sameness," in *Black Feminist Anthropology*, ed. Irma McClaurin, New Brunswick, NJ: Rutgers University Press, 2001, 77–101.
2. Ibid., 78.
3. Ibid., 78, 79.
4. Ibid., 79.
5. Ibid., 80.
6. Ibid., 82.
7. Ibid., 82–83.
8. J. Deotis Roberts, *A Black Political Theology*, Philadelphia, PA: Westminster Press, 1974.
9. See Victor Anderson, *Beyond Ontological Blackness*, New York: Continuum, 1995.
10. *A Black Political Theology*, 75.
11. Ibid., 92.
12. Ibid., 76.
13. Howard Thurman, *Jesus and the Disinherited*, Nashville and New York: Abingdon Press, 1949, 30–31.
14. *A Black Political Theology*, 76.
15. Ibid., 79.
16. Ibid., 89.
17. Ibid., 87.
18. Ibid., 90.
19. Ibid.
20. "Womanist Theology: Black Women's Experience as a Source for Doing Theology, with Special Reference to Christology," in *Black Theology: A Documentary History, Vol. 2*, ed. Cone and Wilmore, 273–289.

21. Ibid., 279.
22. Ibid., 273.
23. bell hooks, *Where We Stand: Class Matters*, New York and London: Routledge, 2000.
24. Ibid., 103.
25. "Womanist Theology: Black Women's Experience as a Source for Doing Theology," 284–285.

4   The Black Church and Pedagogy

1. John S. Mbiti, "Eschatology," in *Biblical Revelation and African Beliefs*, ed. Kwesi Dickson and Paul Ellingworth, Woking, Surrey: Lutterworth, 1969, 159–184.
2. James H. Cone, *The Spirituals and the Blues*, New York: Seabury, 1972, 90.
3. Harold A. Carter, *The Prayer Tradition of Black People*, Valley Forge, PA: Judson Press, 1976, 29.
4. See Martin R. Delaney, *The Condition, Elevation, Emigration and Destiny of the Colored People of the United States, Politically Considered*, Philadelphia, 1852, 38.
5. Albert Raboteau, *Slave Religion*, New York: Oxford University Press, 1978, 213.
6. Ibid., 214.
7. Henry McNeil Turner, "The Voice of Mission," February 1, 1898, cited in Gayraud Wilmore, *Black Religion & Black Radicalism*, Garden City, NJ: Doubleday, 1972, 172.
8. Amy Jacque Garvey, ed. *Philosophy and Opinions of Marcus Garvey, Vol. 1*, New York: Atheneum, 1974, 44.
9. Amy Jacques Garvey, *Garvey and Garveyism*, Kingston: United Printers, 1963. 11–12.
10. *Black Religion and Black Radicalism*, 208.
11. *Garvey and Garveyism*, 134.
12. Ibid.
13. See *New American Standard Bible*.
14. King, *Stride toward Freedom*, 84.
15. Lawrence N. Jones, "The Black Churches: A New Agenda?" *Christian Century*, 96, No. 14, April 18, 1979: 434.
16. Ibid., 437.
17. Charles S. Spivey, Jr., "The Future of the Black Church" in *The Chicago Theological Seminary Register*, 73, No.1, Winter 1983: 50.
18. Ibid, 51.
19. Ibid.
20. C. Eric Lincoln and Lawrence H .Mamiya, *The Black Church in the African American Experience*, Durham, NC: Duke University Press, 1990, 275.

21. C. Eric Lincoln and Lawrence H .Mamiya, *The Black Church in the African American Experience*, Durham, NC: Duke University Press, 1990, 276.
22. Ibid., 278.
23. Ibid.

5 Emancipatory Praxis and Liberation for Oppressors

1. Jurgen Moltmann, "The Liberation of Oppressors," *The Journal of the Interdenominational Theological Center*, 6, No. 2, Spring 1979: 69–82, 69.
2. Ibid.
3. Ibid., 70.
4. Ibid.
5. J.Deotis Roberts, *Liberation and Reconciliation*, Philadelphia, PA: Westminster Press, 1971, 24.
6. Ibid., 24–25.
7. Moltmann, "The Liberation of Oppressors," 70.
8. Ibid., 71.
9. Ibid.
10. Ibid., 72.
11. Ibid.
12. Ibid., 73.
13. Ibid.
14. Shayne Lee, *America's New Preacher: T.D. Jakes*, New York: New York University Press, 2005.
15. James H. Cone, "Black Theology and the Black Church: Where Do We Go From Here?" in *Theology in the Americas* (Documentation Series) Document No. 4, 1978, 8.
16. Moltmann, "The Liberation of Oppressors," 74.
17. Ibid.
18. Ibid., 74–75.
19. Ibid., 75.
20. Ibid.
21. Ibid., 76.
22. Ibid.
23. Ibid., 77.
24. Ibid.
25. Ibid.
26. Ibid.
27. See *New American Standard Bible*.
28. Moltmann, "The Liberation of Oppressors," 77.
29. Ibid.
30. Ibid., 78.
31. Ibid.

32. Ibid.
33. Ibid., 79.
34. Ibid., 80.
35. Ibid., 82.

6   Pedagogy as Celebration

1. See Paul Lehmann, *Ethics in a Christian Context*, San Francisco: Harper &
   Row, 1962. I am grateful to Paul Lehmann who was my teacher at Union
   Theological Seminary for teasing out the distinctions between the rugged and
   the redeemed individual.
2. Katie Geneva Cannon, "Transformative Grace," in *Feminist and Womanist
   Essays in Reformed Dogmatics*, eds. Amy Plantinga Pauw and Serene Jones
   Louisville, London: Westminster John Knox Press, 2006, 139.
3. Ibid., 140.
4. Ibid., 141.
5. Ibid., 143.
6. Ibid., 143–145.
7. Cited, Ibid., 145.
8. Ibid., 147.

Bibliography

Anderson, Victor. *Beyond Ontological Blackness: An Essay on African American Religious and Cultural Criticism.* New York: Continuum, 1995.

Bennett, Lerone Jr. *Before the Mayflower.* Baltimore, MD: Penguin Books, 1973.

Brown, Christopher M. Ed. *Still not Equal.* New York: Peter Lang, 2007.

Cannon, Katie Geneva. *Black Womanist Ethics.* Atlanta: Scholars Press, 1988.

———. "Transformative Grace." In *Feminist and Womanist Essays in Reformed Dogmatics,* Amy Plantinga Pauw and Serene Jones. Eds. Louisville, London: Westminster John Knox Press, 2006, 139.

Carter, Harold A. *The Prayer Tradition of Black People.* Valley Forge, PA:Judson Press, 1976.

Collins, Patricia Hill. *Black Feminist Thought.* New York, London: Routledge, 1991.

———. "Learning from the Outsider Within: The Sociological Significance of Black Feminist Thought." In *Beyond Methodology,* Mary Margaret Fonnow and Judith A.Cook. Eds. Bloomington and Indianapolis, IN: Indiana University Press, 1991, 35–59.

Cone, Cecil Wayne. *The Identity Crisis in Black Theology.* Nashville, TN: AMEC Sunday School Union, 1975.

Cone, James H. *Black Theology and Black Power.* New York: Seabury Press, 1969.

———. "Black Theology and the Black Church: Where Do We Go From Here?" In *Theology in the Americas* (Documentation Series), Document No. 4, 1978, 8.

———. "The Easy Conscience of America's Churches on Race." *Spirituality Justice,* Reprint. Bill Thompson. Ed. January–February 2003.

———. "The Gospel and the Liberation of the Poor." *Christian Century,* February 1, 1981, 162–166.

———. "Introduction." In *Black Theology: A Documentary History, 1966–1979,* James H. Cone, and Gayraud S. Wilmore. Eds. Maryknoll, NY: Orbis Books, 1979.

———. *Martin and Malcolm and America: A Dream or a Nightmare.* Maryknoll, NY: Orbis Books, 1991.

———. *Risks of Faith.* Boston: Beacon Press, 1999.

———. *The Spirituals and the Blues.* New York: Seabury, 1972.

Cone, James H. and Gayraud S. Wilmore. Eds. "Womanist Theology: Black Women's Experience as a Source for Doing Theology." *Black Theology: A*

Documentary History, Vol. 2, 1980–1992, Maryknoll, NY: Orbis Books, 1993.

Delaney, Martin R. *The Condition, Elevation, Emigration and Destiny of the Colored People of the United States, Politically Considered.* Philadelphia, 1852.

Erskine, Noel Leo. *From Garvey to Marley: Rastafari Theology.* Gainesville, FL: University Press of Florida, 2007.

Foster, Michele. *Black Teachers on Teaching.* New York: The New York Press, 1997.

Frederick, Marla F. *Between Sundays.* Berkeley, CA: University of California Press, 2003.

Freire, Paulo. *Teachers as Cultural Workers.* Boulder, CO: Westview Press, 1998.

Gardiner, James J. and J. Deotis Roberts, Sr. Eds. *Quest for a Black Theology.* Philadelphia, PA: Pilgrim Press, 1971.

Garvey, Amy Jacques. *Garvey and Garveyism.* Kingston, Jamaica: United Printers, 1963.

———. Ed. *Philosophy and Opinions of Marcus Garvey, Vol. 1.* New York: Atheneum, 1974.

Gilkes, Cheryl Townsend. *If It Wasn't For the Woman.* Maryknoll, NY: Orbis Books, 2001.

Goately, David Emmanuel. *Were You There?* Maryknoll, NY: Orbis Books, 1996.

Grant, Jacqueline. *White Women's Christ and Black Women's Jesus.* Atlanta: Scholars Press, 1989.

Grant, Jacquelyn. "Black Theology and the Black Woman." In *Black Theology*, Cone, and Wilmore. Eds., 420.

Green, Maxine. *Teacher as Stranger* Belmont, California: Wadsworth Publishing Company, 1973.

hooks, bell. *Teaching to Transgress.* New York and London: Routledge, 1994.

———. *Where We Stand: Class Matters.* New York: Routledge, 2000.

Hopkins, Dwight N., and Anthony B. Pinn. Eds. *Loving the Body.* New York: Palgrave Macmillan, 2006.

Hopkins, Dwight N., and George Cummings. *Cut Loose Your Stammering Tongue.* Maryknoll, NY: Orbis Books, 1991.

James H. Cone. "A Black Theology of Liberation." Philadelphia and New York: J.B. Lippincott Company, 1970.

Jones, Lawrence N. "The Black Churches: A New Agenda?" *Christian Century*, 96, No.14. April 18, 1979.

King, Martin Luther Jr. "The Ethical Demands for Integration." In *A Testament of Hope*, Washington, Ed., 122.

———. "Facing the Challenge of a New Age." *A Testament of Hope: The Essential Writings of Martin Luther King, Jr.*, James M. Washington, Ed. San Francisco: Harper & Row, 1986. 140.

———. "I See the Promised Land." In *A Testament of Hope*, Washington, Ed. 122.

———. "Remaining Awake through a Great Revolution." In *A Testament of Hope*, Washington, Ed., 269.

———. *Stride Toward Freedom.* San Francisco : Harper & Row, 1958.

———. *The Trumpet of Conscience* New York: Harper & Row, 1967.

———. "Where Do We Go From Here." In *A Testament of Hope*, Washington, Ed., 246.

Lee, Shayne. *America's New Preacher: T.D. Jakes*. New York: New York University Press, 2005.

Lehmann, Paul. *Ethics in a Christian Context*. San Francisco: Harper & Row, 1962.

Lincoln, Eric C., and Lawrence H. Mamiya. *The Black Church in the African American Experience*. Durham, NC: Duke University Press, 1990.

Mbiti, John S. "Eschatology." In *Biblical Revelation and African Beliefs*, Kwesi Dickson and Paul Ellingworth. Eds. Woking, Surrey: Lutterworth, 1969.

Mitchell, Henry H. *Black Church Beginnings*. Grand Rapids, MI: William B. Eerdmans, 2004.

Moltmann, Jurgen. "The Liberation of Oppressors." *The Journal of the Interdenominational Theological Center*, 6, No. 2, Spring 1979, 69–82.

Moore Mullino, Mary Elizabeth. *Teaching From the Hear*. Minneapolis, MN: Fortress Press, 1991.

National Committee of Negro Churchmen, "Black Power Statement." *The New York Times*, July 31, 1966.

Pinn, Anthony B. *Terror and Triumph: The Nature of Black Religion*. Minneapolis, MN: Fortress, 2003.

———. *Why Lord?* New York: Continuum, 1999.

Pobee, John. Ed. *Towards Viable Theological Education*. Geneva: WCC Publications, 1997.

Raboteau, Albert. *Slave Religion*. New York: Oxford University Press, 1978.

Reddie, Anthony G. *Black Theology in Transatlantic Dialogue*. New York: Palgrave Macmillam, 2006.

———. *Nobodies to Somebodies*. London: Epworth Press, 2003.

Riggs, Marcia Y. *Awake, Arise & Act*. Cleveland, Ohio: Pilgrim Press, 1994.

Roberts, J. Deotis. *A Black Political Theology*. Philadelphia, PA: Westminster Press, 1974.

———. "Liberating Theological Education: Can Our Seminaries Be Saved?" *Christian Century*, 100, No. 4, February 1983, 98, 113–116.

———. *Liberation and Reconciliation*. Louisville: Westminster, John Knox Press, 2005.

Ross, Rosetta E. *Witnessing & Testifying*. Minneapolis, MN: Fortress Press, 2003.

Seymore, Jack L., and Donald E. Miller. Eds. *Theological Approaches to Christian Education*. Nashville, TN: Abington Press, 1990.

Simmons, Kimberly Eison. "A Passion for Sameness." In *Black Feminist Anthropology*, Irma McClaurin, Ed. New Brunswich, NJ: Rutgers University Press, 2001, 77–101.

Smith, Wallace Charles. *The Church in the Life of the Black Family*. Valley Forge, PA.: Judson Press, 1985.

Snarey, John R., and Vanessa Siddle Walker. *Race-ing Moral Formation*. New York: Teachers College Press, 2004.

Spivey, Charles S. Jr. "The Future of the Black Church." *The Chicago Theological Seminary Register*, 73, No. 1, Winter 1983, 50.

Thurman, Howard. *Jesus and the Disinherited*. Nashville, TN and New York: Abingdon Press, 1949.

Trifonas, Peter Pericles. Ed. *Pedagogies of Difference*. New York: RoutledgeFalmer, 2003.

Turner, Henry McNeil. "The Voice of Mission." February 1, 1898, cited in Gayraud Wilmore, *Black Religion & Black Radicalism*. Garden City: Doubleday, 1972.

West, Cornel. "Black Theology and Human Identity." In *Black Faith and Public Talk*, Dwight N. Hopkins, Ed. Waco, TX: Baylor University Press, 2007, 15–16.

Williams, Preston N. "The Ethics of Black Power." In *Quest for a Black Theology*, Gardiner and Roberts, Eds., 85.

Wilmore, Gayraud S. *Black Religion and Black Radicalism*. Maryknoll, NY: Orbis Books, 2003.

Index